D0714746

Copyright

interpreting the law for
libraries, archives and
information services

Copyright

interpreting the law for
libraries, archives and
information services

FIFTH EDITION

Graham P. Cornish

 facet publishing

Published by Facet Publishing
7 Ridgmount Street, London WC1E 7AE
www.facetpublishing.co.uk

Facet Publishing is wholly owned by CILIP: the Chartered Institute of Library
and Information Professionals.

British Library Cataloguing in Publication Data
A catalogue record for this book is available from the British Library.

ISBN 978-1-85604-664-0

First published 1990
Second edition 1997
Third edition 1999
Third revised edition 2001
Fourth edition 2004
This fifth edition 2009

Text printed on FSC accredited material.

Mixed Sources
Product group from well-managed
forests and other controlled sources
www.fsc.org Cert no. SA-COC-1565
© 1996 Forest Stewardship Council
FSC

Typeset from author's files in 10/14pt American Garamond and Function
by Facet Publishing.

Printed and made in Great Britain by MPG Books Group, UK.

Contents

Author's note

This book tries to set out the basics of UK copyright law, concentrating on those areas which may affect librarians and archivists in their daily work. Some areas have not been dealt with at length if they do not relate directly to libraries and archives (although the boundaries are becoming increasingly blurred by changes in management and the way information is delivered) and the whole area of design and patents is left to others far more competent to deal with them in those areas where they impinge on the work of libraries. Neither is it intended as a scholarly textbook but rather as a working tool for the practitioner who is faced with actual situations which need to be resolved in an informed and sensible way. Therefore references to case law or even specific clauses of the legislation are not included. It can be used as a desktop reference work for anyone planning library, archive and information services or kept at the enquiry desk to help decide what can, or cannot, be done for a reader. The author's hope is that it will be as helpful to junior counter staff as to senior managers. It is also aimed at all types of library, archive and information service, whether public, academic, government or private. Attention is given to the different legal situations in which various libraries function. As would be expected, the book focuses on UK law, which it aims to interpret, and the answers found here should never be assumed to apply in other countries. Nevertheless, many of the questions raised are equally valid in any part of the world and should help professionals in other countries to address the issues facing their own libraries.

As libraries, archives and information providers increasingly move towards exploiting their collections or providing new information resources, there is a need to look at what rights libraries and others enjoy when they create a work as well as when they wish to use something. Digitization programmes in particular raise many challenging questions and some of these will be dealt with in this book.

It is organized on a question-and-answer basis to simplify searching for particular problems and their possible solutions. Because of this there is a small amount of repetition between sections. This is quite deliberate to avoid unnecessary 'see also' comments, which tend to confuse or bewilder the user. Obviously not every possible question can be answered but every effort has been made to anticipate those which arise most often. The feedback from many users of previous editions of this book has been most useful in expanding and amplifying some of the paragraphs in this edition. The law is there not to deal in specific terms with any and every possible situation but to provide the framework within which decisions can be made in specific circumstances. There are always 'grey' areas of interpretation or circumstance when the law will be unclear. Where this is the case, the book tries to offer guidance rather than provide a definite answer, as this is just not always possible. Although some of the legislation is still quite new, other elements have been in place long enough to make it possible to give some further guidance in areas which were 'fuzzy' when the first edition was prepared in 1989. It should be remembered that what the law does not allow can often be done with the copyright owner's consent through an appropriate licence. Therefore, where the book says that the law prevents something, librarians and archivists should first check to see what kind of licence, if any, their institution holds for copying beyond the stated limits. For this reason a chapter on licences has been included in the certain knowledge that it will soon become out of date in such a fast-moving area. In a book of this kind it is not possible to say exactly what existing licences allow as they will differ between different types of institution and will change with time but general indications have been given as guidance.

The author has worked in the field of copyright since 1983 and advised the British Library on copyright matters for 18 years, taking part in many of the discussions which helped to shape the library profession's reaction to the new law and the many Statutory Instruments which have followed the main legislation. He was involved in many similar discussions in Brussels and Luxembourg when the EU introduced a series of directives which have profoundly changed some aspects of UK law. He has been a member of groups and committees dealing with copyright matters and has lectured and run seminars on copyright law both in the UK and abroad. He was also involved in a number of initiatives designing and implementing Electronic Copyright Management Systems (ECMS) which now play a major role in the management of information work world wide. He now works as an independent advisor and trainer in all aspects of copyright under the label ©opyright Circle. The wealth of information and opinion gathered from these contacts has been used to compile this book but it must be remembered that it is written by a librarian trying to understand the law, not a lawyer trying to understand libraries!

Graham P. Cornish

Disclaimer

While the advice and information contained in this book are believed to be true and accurate at the date of going to press, neither the author nor CILIP can accept any legal responsibility or liability for any errors or omissions that may be made.

Acknowledgements

Nobody knows everything about copyright. Consequently, anyone who writes a book on the subject must be indebted to others working in the field. This is certainly true of this author and I would like to thank particularly Tim Padfield of The National Archives (TNA) for his wisdom on every aspect of archives; Charles Oppenheim of Loughborough University for his challenging alternative interpretations of the law, various members of the Libraries & Archives Copyright Alliance (LACA) and, above all, the many people who have taken part in the numerous copyright workshops throughout the country at which I have taught and whose questions have so enriched this edition.

My thanks also go to my friend and long-standing colleague Stella Pilling for proof-reading my text.

Graham P. Cornish

OUEE	Open University Educational Enterprises
PLR	Public Lending Right
PPL	Phonographic Performances Ltd
PRS	Performing Right Society
SI	Statutory Instrument
TNA	The National Archives
TRIPS	Trade-Related Intellectual Property Rights
UCC	Universal Copyright Convention
USGPO	United States Government Printing Office
VAT	value added tax
VIP	visually impaired person
VLE	virtual learning environment
WIPO	World Intellectual Property Organization

Introduction

The 1988 Copyright, Designs and Patents Act (CDPA) and the many subsequent Statutory Instruments which interpret and modify it differ substantially from the one of 1956. However, some aspects of this old Act still apply to some materials, as do some clauses of the 1911 Act, so it should not be ignored completely. Many definitions have changed, new rights have been introduced, lending and rental now play a much more prominent role in the law as it relates to libraries than previously and the right of communication to the public by electronic means needs careful scrutiny. Licensing as a concept is now also a major feature of information delivery but it was in its infancy in 1988.

The introduction of new legislation often has the effect of heightening awareness of the subject, making people more keen to know their rights and privileges and generally creating an atmosphere of extreme caution in case anyone puts a foot wrong and ends up in court. While this is a good thing, nobody should become too paranoid. Although there has been a recent tendency for copyright infringement cases to be heard in criminal courts, this is usually where important commercial considerations apply, such as republishing or reproduction in bulk for commercial purposes. Criminal proceedings may also be taken for circumventing or tampering with electronic rights management systems. Most infringements of copyright by individuals are dealt with through the civil courts so the rights owner must take legal proceedings if it is thought an infringement has taken place. As there are no cases at present involving libraries as such, it would be reasonable to assume that a similar route would be taken, given that libraries are not, or should not be, involved in mass reproduction for commercial gain!

The Act and its supplementary legislation also set the stage for a completely new approach to the use of copyright material. We all know what the law says (even if we do not always know what it means!) so there is now the necessity to develop services outside the exceptions which the Copyright Act makes by talking to the licensing agencies and other rights owners' organizations to negotiate use of material in return for royalties. Those working in the information industries should not lose sight of this as a real way forward when the law inhibits the introduction of new services without the owners' consent. Licences granted by copyright owners can also override the limitations set by the law.

1.3   **Why is copyright important for libraries and archives?**

Libraries are in a unique position as custodians of copyright material. They have the duty to care for, and allow access to, other people's copyright works. This places special responsibilities on all those working in libraries, archives and the information world generally. We practise our profession by using this property so we should take all possible steps to protect it, while at the same time ensuring that the rights and privileges of our users and our profession are also safeguarded.

1.4   **Why is copyright so often ignored by users?**

Because it is such an intangible thing, there is often a temptation to ignore it. Those who take this approach forget that they, too, own copyright in their own creations and would feel quite angry if this were abused by others. Some of the restrictions placed on use by the law may seem petty or trivial but they are designed to allow some use of copyright material without unduly harming the interests of the creator (author).

1.5   **Is copyright valuable in terms of money?**

Copyright is, in the UK, primarily a property right intended to protect the rights of those who create works of various kinds. The protection is to prevent exploitation of their works by others. It follows that copyright cannot exist by itself but only within the work which has been created. For this reason we say that copyright 'subsists' rather than exists.

1.6   **So, is copyright just about cash?**

No, authors also need to protect their personal rights, regardless of money. These rights are outlined in Section 3.

1.7   **What is the latest legislation?**

There are two Acts of Parliament which are crucial to copyright. These are the Copyright, Designs and Patents Act (CDPA) 1988, which came into force on 1 August 1989, and the Copyright (Visually Impaired Persons) Act 2002 which came into force on 31 October 2003. The CDPA has to be read in conjunction with a number of subsequent Statutory Instruments and the supporting Regulations. There are a number of these, but the Statutory Instruments which affect libraries and archives most are:

SI 89/816 Copyright, Designs and Patents Act 1988 (Commencement No.1) Order

SI 89/1012 The Copyright (Recordings of Folksongs for Archives) (Designated Bodies) Order 1989

SI 89/1098 The Copyright (Material Open to Public Inspection) (International Organisations) Order 1989

SI 89/1099 The Copyright (Material Open to Public Inspection) (Marking of Copies of Maps) Order 1989

SI 89/1212 The Copyright (Librarians and Archivists) (Copying of Copyright Materials) Regulations 1989

SI 89/2510 The Copyright (Recording for Archives of Designated Class of Broadcasts and Cable Programmes) (Designated Bodies) (No.2) Order 1989

SI 92/3233 The Copyright (Computer Programs) Regulations 1992

SI 95/3297 The Duration of Copyright and Rights in Performances Regulations 1995

SI 96/2967 The Copyright and Related Rights Regulations 1996

SI 97/3032 The Copyright and Rights in Databases Regulations 1997

SI 2003/2498 Copyright and Related Rights Regulations 2003

SI 2005/223 The Copyright (Educational Establishments) Order 2005

SI 2006/18 The Performances (Moral Rights, etc.) Regulations 2006

SI 2006/346 The Artist's Resale Right Regulations 2006

SI 2008/677 The Copyright and Performances (Application to Other Countries) Order 2008.

Note that the texts of all this legislation can be found on the OPSI website, so extracts are not reproduced in this book. Go to www.opsi.gov.uk for the text of Acts of Parliament and Statutory Instruments.

1.8 It is important to note that a number of defective Statutory Instruments were drawn up for this Act and never implemented.

The above list includes all those of direct relevance to libraries and archives. Other SIs with the same title but different numbering were replaced by those listed and the earlier ones should be ignored. This also applies to some SIs which became out of date and were effectively updated with replacements. It should also be noted that a number of terms used in the legislation are not defined. It is also worth noting that SIs that put in place what the Act says simply give more detail than the Act itself can do. SIs that implement European Directives are far more complicated and may remove parts of the Act, modify other parts and will certainly introduce new sections and clauses. So never just look at the original Act itself.

1.9 **So, if I have all this legislation in front of me, can I work out what the law means?**

No! In addition to the many Statutory Instruments, you need to bear in mind that (a) the language in the Act is full of undefined terms and (b) case law frequently changes the way we understand the meaning of the Act.

1.10 **How can I keep up with the changes to the law?**

There are some suggestions in Appendix 1 to help with this problem.

1.11 **Which terms are undefined?**

The following words and phrases crop up frequently but are never defined: commercial research, fair dealing, librarian, original, periodical, reasonable (and reasonably), substantial (and substantially).

1.12 **Does the law apply to the whole of the UK?**

Yes, but remember that the Isle of Man and the Channel Islands are not part of the UK. Most (but not quite all) of the 1988 Act does not apply to the Channel Islands, which are still subject to either the 1956 Act or even parts of the 1911 Act. The Isle of Man passed its own copyright legislation in 1991, so the copyright part of this Act (Part 1) does not apply there. The Manx legislation is sufficiently similar to UK law not to cause major problems. Also the Isle of Man is now covered by the database legislation. In addition, some aspects of remedies for owners relating to infringement and some of the criminal aspects of copyright are handled differently in Scotland because of the different way that Scots law works in these areas. It is to be hoped that users of this book never have to investigate these!

1.13 **Any other catches?**

Yes, some phrases and words mean different things in different parts of the law. For example 'making available to the public' has several different meanings, as does 'publish'.

Section 2
What is covered by copyright?

2.1 What things are covered by copyright?

Virtually anything that is written, expressed in graphic form or recorded in any way, or anything that can be made by a human being, but not usually things made by a mechanical process. The law divides these items into various classes and all aspects of them are dealt with separately in the following pages.

2.2 Does absolutely anything in these groups qualify for copyright?

No. There are three tests to qualify for copyright and any work must pass all three. They are that the work must be original, recorded and created by a qualifying person.

2.3 What does 'original' mean?

The law does not say, but the idea is that to be protected the author must have contributed quite a lot of their own ideas or skills to the making of the work. Works that are merely trivial will not qualify, as they are not original. Anything that is merely a copy of something that already exists cannot be protected by copyright as a new work.

2.4 What constitutes trivial?

This is not defined, but a primitive doodle or a simple 'x' would not qualify although what is 'simple' and what is not is open to debate!

2.5 When does a work based on another work become original?

When sufficient time, effort, technical skills and knowledge have been used to make it reasonably clear that the work is a new one and not merely a slavish copy.

Example: If you write your own poem about Jack and Jill, it is protected. If you simply reproduce the well known nursery rhyme with one or two minor changes, that is not original and not protected – but if you photocopy/scan the poem the typographical arrangement may be (see paragraphs 4.88 onwards).

2.6   What about digitization and the images which it produces?

This is an area where the law is unclear. Generally speaking, it is held that if the work is digitized using a scanner and there is no human intervention (like a photocopy or producing a pdf file that cannot be manipulated), then there is unlikely to be any new copyright work created. So a mere scanned copy may not be protected by copyright but an image that has had a lot of work carried out on it to enhance its appearance or correct the text or which changes the colouring (using OCR-type technology) probably will be protected.

2.7   So, if the library digitizes some old parts of its collection, can it benefit at all from copyright?

If the images are enhanced, probably. But even if they are not, the actual collection of images may qualify for database right (see Section 9) if they are organized in a systematic and methodical way.

2.8   What does 'recorded' mean?

Fixed in some way such as writing using any form of notation or code, stored in a computer system, recorded on a disc (vinyl, CD(-ROM)) or on a film (including video and DVD). A live performance which is not recorded or videoed, for example, would not attract copyright because it ceases to exist as soon as it is delivered. There is nothing to show what it contained or what it was like so it cannot be copied, nor can the person who delivered it show what was in it.

2.9   Can copyright subsist even if the original work has disappeared or been destroyed?

Yes. If, for example, a painting was photographed and then destroyed, there would still be copyright in the original painting, even though it did not exist, through the existence of the photograph.

2.10   Which works qualify for copyright protection?

The person claiming to be the author must be a UK citizen or a citizen of a country where UK works are protected in the same way as in the UK (see paragraphs 12.1 and following). A complete list of these countries is given in the relevant Statutory Instruments listed in Section 1. Also anyone carrying out work for the Crown, Parliament, the United Nations or the Organization of American States has that work protected as if it were published in the UK, even if the author is a national of a country not otherwise covered by these arrangements.

See also paragraphs 4.101 and following.

If there is no author the work must have been published in a country which protects works in the same way as the UK.

2.11 Is there copyright in facts?

No. A fact is a fact and cannot be protected as such. However, the way in which information about facts is presented is protected. Similarly, ideas are not protected, only the expression of them.

Example: Times of trains are facts and nobody can prevent you from publishing information that trains leave at certain times for particular places. What is protected is the layout of the timetable and the actual typography. So you might make this information available by including it in a brochure about a tourist attraction but it would be an infringement to reproduce the timetable and reprint it in the brochure.

2.12 Is the title of a book or journal article protected by copyright?

Rarely. Such titles are statements of fact – they tell you what the book or article is called – and cannot therefore be protected unless they are so complex that they become a literary work in their own right or are registered as a trademark. In this case the problem would arise only if the 'make-up' of the new work looked so like the first work that one could be mistaken for the other. How many journals called *Impact* or *Update* do you know?

2.13 What about works which are illegal, such as pornography?

Just because a work is pornographic, libellous or irreligious does not mean it is not protected by copyright. On the other hand, courts have sometimes refused to uphold copyright in such works where a claim for infringement has occurred. The problem is, as always in such matters, that what is pornographic today may be entirely acceptable tomorrow. Thus there will be copyright in such works but it may be difficult to enforce.

2.14 Are things like trademarks and logos protected by copyright?

Yes. A logo is an artistic work and a trademark may well be an artistic work and/or a literary work as well. It is quite possible for a trademark to go out of copyright but still be a trademark, as trademarks can last indefinitely. Therefore it could be legal to copy an old trademark, provided it was not used to market a similar product. For example, it might be possible to illustrate a book on advertising with pictures of out-of-copyright trademarks, but not to use the same trademark for products sold in a museum shop showing retail life 100 years ago.

2.15 What about foreign materials? Are they covered by copyright?

It depends on whether the country of origin of the author, or the country where the work was first published, is a member of one of the major international treaties on copyright. If they are, then their material is treated as if it came from the UK (but see paragraphs 4.101 and following for some limits on how long copyright lasts). If they do not come from one of these countries, then they do not enjoy copyright protection. See Statutory Instrument 2008/677 for a complete list.

2.16 Are any works excepted from the usual copyright protection?

Yes. The King James Version of the Bible (also referred to as the Authorized Version), the Book of Common Prayer of the Church of England (BCP) and Sir James Barrie's *Peter Pan* all enjoy special protection outside normal copyright limitations. The Authorized Version of the Bible and the BCP are printed under patents issued by the Crown and are therefore in perpetual copyright. This does not extend to modern versions, which must be treated as published works which are anonymous, whatever one's personal theological view! The Authorized Version of the Bible and BCP cannot be copied, as they are outside copyright law. Permission is usually given for small quotations in publications, and photocopying of various portions for research or private study or reading in church or chapel is usually allowed. In the case of *Peter Pan*, the Copyright Act brought in perpetual copyright in this play for the benefit of the Hospital for Sick Children, Great Ormond Street, London, provided it remains as a hospital. The Hospital owned the copyright, which expired on 31 December 1987, and obtained a considerable revenue from it. Parliament decided to continue this privilege and any commercial publication or performance of the work attracts a royalty for the Hospital. This is a form of compulsory licensing for a work now out of copyright. As the Act did not come into force until 1 August 1989, any act of copying, commercial publication or performance carried out between 31 December 1987 and 31 July 1989 was not an infringement. The play cannot be publicly performed without royalty payment to the Hospital for Sick Children. As this law applies only to the UK it causes considerable confusion for the film industry, which is free to exploit the work outside the UK but not to import products derived from it into the UK without a licence from the Hospital.

In addition, some items, such as patents, qualify technically for copyright, but an international agreement between patent offices has waived all protection of patents for non-commercial copying.

Section 3
Rights and limitations

3.1 What is the difference between authorship and ownership?

Authors and owners may or may not be the same person. They enjoy different rights, so this distinction is important. As authors are defined differently for different types of work, they will be dealt with separately under each heading. However, despite some variations, their moral rights are similar in most circumstances, so they will be covered in this section. This section sets out who the owner is and what the owner is entitled to do exclusively in law. The rights enjoyed by authors are called 'moral rights' and are generally very weak in UK law. On the other hand, owners enjoy a whole range of rights which are economic in nature. The limitations to these rights are dealt with in Section 4.

Moral rights
3.2 What are moral rights?

Moral rights are designed to protect the idea that anything created contains an element of 'self' in it. Therefore the author ought to be able to protect certain aspects of a work. Although the law is complex in this area and most library services may not think they have major concerns with moral rights, the growth of electronic information sources, Open Archives, Creative Commons and similar systems makes an understanding of moral rights important for all information services.

3.3 What are these rights?

Essentially they give the author the right not to have their work subjected to derogatory treatment.

3.4 What constitutes derogatory treatment?

Basically, authors have a right to prevent their work being distorted by additions, deletions or changes to its meaning. They also have the right not to have works they did not create attributed to them and to prevent anyone else claiming to be the author of their work. They also have the right to prevent their work being used in a way that would bring their reputation into disrepute.

3.5   What about making sure their name is included in a work?

This is not, surprisingly, an automatic right of the author. It applies in certain contexts only and will be dealt with under each type of copyright material in the following sections. In summary, it applies only to authors of monographs, producers and directors of films and artists whose work is to be exhibited in public.

3.6   Do all authors enjoy moral rights?

No. Anyone who creates anything as part of their employment forfeits virtually all moral rights to their employer. See paragraphs 3.14 and following.

3.7   Do moral rights last for the same length of time as other rights?

Yes, but with one important exception. The right not to have works falsely attributed to oneself lasts for only 20 years from the end of the year in which the person dies.

Ownership of copyright

3.8   Who owns copyright?

Ownership of copyright is a complex question. Copyright is a property and can be disposed of in the same way as other property, so ownership is not always easy to identify. The author may have assigned the copyright to someone else. It may have been sold to a publisher, given to someone else, left to someone in a will or automatically transferred to an employer, the Crown or Parliament. In 1996 the law changed, extending copyright protection in many cases from 50 to 70 years after death. This gave rise to 'extended' copyright (where 20 years has been added on to existing copyright) and 'revived' copyright (where a work was out of copyright because the author had been dead for more than 50 years but, because they had been dead for fewer than 70 years, copyright came back into force).

3.9   Is the copyright in a work one single piece of property or can it be broken up?

Copyright is a quite complicated bundle of rights (see paragraph 3.32 and following) and these can be assigned or licensed to different people. Also, different rights can be licensed to different people. For example, the author of a book may license publication in hardback to one publisher, paperback to another, distribution in different parts of the world to different publishers again, making of an audio version to yet another company and film rights to someone else entirely. Rights can also be licensed for a limited period, so that one person may have one bundle of rights for 10 years then acquire a licence for them for a further 30 years and so on. This is particularly important for works made into films or plays, musicals, operas and ballets.

3.10   Are there any rules for transferring copyright?

Yes, an assignment of copyright by which the owner passes over some or all of their rights *exclusively* for a specified period, must be in writing. Failure to have this in writing means that there is no transfer of copyright. This is very important for contracts.

3.11   What is the difference between an assignment and a licence?

An assignment transfers the management of copyright to someone else, usually for a given period and for specified purposes. During that time the original owner cannot exercise any of the rights transferred under the assignment. Licences are quite different. They do not transfer any rights but allow other people to share in the rights of the owner (for example, to copy a work), but the original owner retains all their rights and the licensee does not gain any rights, only permissions. This is a feature of copyright management that is quite different from managing other types of property.

3.12   Someone must start the ownership process. Who owns copyright first?

Copyright is usually owned first of all by the author.

3.13   Why is the author 'usually' the first owner?

Because there are different rules depending on employment or commissioning.

3.14   How does employment come into ownership?

If authors create a work as part of their job, then their employer is usually the owner. However, there can be a contract between employer and employee which states the opposite (i.e. the copyright remains with the employee). See the notes on commissioned works in the following paragraphs. There are special arrangements for Crown and Parliamentary copyright (see paragraphs 3.27 and following). Also, the author is differently defined for different classes of works, such as films and sound recordings. Most of the legislation is actually about the rights enjoyed by the owner of copyright rather than by the author. For this reason most authors' economic rights are referred to as 'owner's rights'.

3.15 Supposing the work was commissioned?

If the work was commissioned after 1 August 1989, the copyright is owned by the author. Before that date, copyright in commissioned paintings, engravings and photographs is usually the property of the person who paid for the commission. Copyright in other types of commissioned works remains with the person creating the work. As with works created as part of employment, a contract in writing can transfer copyright to the commissioner.

3.16 Does 'commissioned' mean the author had to be paid?

Yes, but this is important now only for artistic works mentioned in the last paragraph.

3.17 What about documents such as minutes of meetings for clubs, societies and churches when the secretary is not employed but is a volunteer?

The most probable situation is that, although the secretary may have put their name on the minutes, the right to exploit those minutes belongs to the club or church. They would enjoy the equity in them even though the secretary could rightly claim to be the author.

3.18 Supposing a library owns an original work such as a manuscript. Does the library own the copyright?

No. It is important to distinguish between the object and the copyright, which subsists in it. The library may own the manuscript but the copyright is still owned by the author or the person to whom it has been assigned, so the library has no right to reproduce the manuscript, except as allowed by the exceptions in the Copyright Act. However, the library may enjoy other rights over the manuscript under publication right (see paragraphs 4.91 and following).

3.19 Who owns the copyright in a work deposited with a library or archive?

There is a special additional exception for unpublished works. When an author leaves their unpublished manuscripts or other materials to a library, archive or museum as a bequest and their will does not specify any other arrangements, the presumption is that the copyright is also transferred to the library, archive or museum. They may specify differently in the will and, if they do, this will affect the way the unpublished material can be used. If the work is deposited by the author during their lifetime or deposited by the family but copyright is not assigned to the library or archive, then copyright remains with the author or their heirs and successors.

3.20 Can the library acquire the copyright?

Yes. When it buys a manuscript, painting, etc. it is possible to buy the copyright as well. Again, this must be under contract in writing. Glasgow City Council owns the copyright in the painting by Salvador Dali called *Christ of St John of the Cross* because it bought it with the painting.

3.21 Who owns the copyright in a letter?

The author, that is, the person who wrote the letter, not the archive which holds the letter.

3.22 Why does the person who received the letter not own it?

Because copyright belongs to the person who creates the work. The letter itself does belong to the person who received it, who was given it by the writer. But the copyright still belongs to the writer, not the recipient, of the letter.

3.23 What about a letter sent to the editor of a newspaper or journal?

Technically the copyright still belongs to the writer of the letter although, by sending the letter to the editor in the first place, there is a presumption that the writer wished it to be published and therefore the editor has an *implied* licence to publish. This does not give the editor or the publisher any other rights over the use of the letter.

3.24 Who owns the copyright in a periodical issue?

Each author of an article in a periodical issue owns the copyright in that article, but the publisher owns the copyright in the issue as a whole, including the typographical arrangement (see paragraphs 4.88 and following).

Example: Someone writes an article for a periodical. Unless they sign an agreement to the contrary, they retain the copyright in the article and have the right to have it published elsewhere. But they do not have the right simply to photocopy the article as first published and have it republished in that form. This would infringe the typographical copyright of the publisher. Nor do they have the right to make copies of the whole periodical issue. For the same reason, the author cannot simply make multiple photocopies of the article for friends and colleagues.

3.25 Who owns 'extended copyright'?

Essentially the person who owned the copyright immediately before the extended copyright came into force (see paragraph 3.8 and following above).

3.26 Who owns 'revived copyright'?

The person who owned the copyright immediately before it expired. If that person is dead, or the body owning the copyright has ceased to exist, then the copyright is owned by the personal representatives of the author (see paragraph 3.8 and following above).

3.27 Who owns Crown copyright?

Crown copyright is explained in more detail at paragraphs 4.85 and following. Technically, the Crown. However, Crown copyright is administered by HMSO, which, although now privatized, still has a residual responsibility to administer copyright owned by the Crown.

3.28 Who owns the copyright in a Parliamentary bill or Act of Parliament?

The copyright in a bill belongs to whichever House introduced the bill first. When the bill becomes an Act it becomes Crown copyright. The copyright in other materials belongs to whichever House first commissioned the work to be done.

3.29 Supposing a work is out of print. Does the publisher still own the copyright?

This will depend on the contract between the author and the publisher but, generally speaking, copyright in a work reverts to the author if the work goes out of print and the publisher has no plans to reprint or republish the work. However, the publisher will retain the copyright in the typography of the work (see paragraphs 4.88 and following).

3.30 **Who owns the copyright in children's work in schools?**

Despite the general myth that it is owned by the school, the child who creates anything in school owns the rights in it and it cannot be used for any purpose without the child's (or guardian's) permission.

3.31 **So what about published children's poems or pictures in magazines or school brochures?**

Permission must be sought from the child or guardian.

3.32 **What rights does the law give the copyright owner?**

Copyright law gives the owner exclusive rights to do certain things to or with the copyright material. Nobody else is entitled to do these things. There are seven basic rights:

- to copy the work
- to issue copies to the public
- to perform, show or play the work in public
- to adapt or translate the work
- to rent or lend the work
- to communicate the work to the public by electronic means
- to make the work available by electronic means.

Each of these rights will be examined under the appropriate type of work. Those who own rights in databases or performances have a different set of rights.

3.33 **Are these absolute rights or do other people have some rights to use the material as well?**

They are not absolute because they are limited by (a) quantity, (b) time, (c) purpose and (d) certain exemptions given to user groups. Each of these limitations will be examined under the appropriate type of work. But it is important to note that the limitations set for use of copyright material are exceptions to the rights of owners and not rights enjoyed by users.

All rights also have limitations in their exercise. The law limits these exclusive rights of copyright owners in a number of ways and this section should be interpreted in the light of what is said later about other people also being allowed to do certain acts. It is these exceptions which form the bulk of this book.

Quantity

3.34   Is the whole and every little bit of a work protected?

No. Copyright is limited by excluding from protection less than a substantial part of a work. So if less than a substantial part is used or copied there is no infringement except in certain areas.

3.35   What constitutes a substantial part?

Substantial is one of those undefined words. What is clear is that it is a question not just of quantity but of quality as well.

Example: Someone copies the recommendations and conclusions (three paragraphs) from a 70-page technical report. This is almost certainly a substantial part. Similarly, four bars of a symphony could constitute a substantial part because they encapsulate the theme music of the whole work. In one case 30 seconds from a one-hour broadcast was considered a substantial part.

3.36   So are there any guidelines on quantity?

Not really. Each case must be a matter of professional judgement.

Time and purpose

3.37   Does copyright last for ever?

No, but the rules relating to just how long it does last are very complex. They will be dealt with for each type of copyright material in the following sections.

3.38   For what purposes can copyright material be used without asking permission?

The law gives several main reasons:

- fair dealing
- public administration
- temporary copies.

These will be dealt with for each type of copyright material in the following sections.

User groups

3.39   **Are any exceptions made for particular user groups or needs?**

The law gives special exceptions and privileges to three user groups:

- those working in or undertaking education
- libraries and their users
- visually impaired people.

Orphan works

3.40   **What if the copyright owner cannot be identified or found?**

This gives rise to what are currently referred to as 'orphan works'. In other words, works for which it is not possible to identify who either the author or the publisher actually was, or for which they can be identified but neither they nor their successors can be traced. In these circumstances the best advice is to make all reasonable enquiries to find their whereabouts but, if all fails, then it is a matter of judgement whether to go ahead and copy/publish/digitize the work or not do any of those things in case the copyright owner comes out of the woodwork. This is a risk assessment exercise which must be undertaken in each circumstance and in relation to each work. Clearly, the risks involved in copying/publishing a local photograph will be different from doing the same with a drawing by a famous artist.

These questions will also be dealt with for each type of copyright material in the following sections.

Section 4
Literary, dramatic and musical works

4.1 **Why are these three grouped together?**

Because they are all treated in a similar way under the Copyright Act, although there are some differences for some specific areas. In addition, a printed text also has a copyright in the typographical arrangement of the work concerned, regardless of the copyright status of the content. Any literary work which will also qualify as a database is subject to special rules. See Section 9 for details.

Definitions
Literary works

4.2 **What is a literary work?**

The term 'literary work' includes anything that is written in any form, such as books, journals, technical reports and manuscripts and also covers any works that are spoken or sung. It also includes compilations (where these do not qualify as databases) as well as computer programs and text stored electronically. So the words of a popular song are protected as a literary work; the music is treated separately (see 'musical works'). The handwritten notes of an author are protected just as much as the final printed book.

4.3 **Does 'literary' mean it has to be good quality literature?**

No. Copyright law says almost nothing about the quality or content of the work, although case law shows that trivial works are not eligible for protection. 'Literary' means anything which is written, spoken or sung which has been recorded, whether in writing or some other way. The use of any notation or code counts as 'written'. This is why a computer program is considered a literary work in legal terms.

4.4 **What about books or articles written in scripts like Japanese, Chinese or Arabic that many people cannot read?**

This makes no difference. They meet the criterion of written in a notation or code.

Just because some people cannot read them it does not mean that others can't!

4.5 **What about databases? Are these covered by copyright?**

They may sometimes be covered by copyright but they are definitely covered by database right as a separate type of work. See Section 9 for details.

4.6 **Are bibliographic records covered by copyright?**

This is a difficult question and has never been clarified in law. The question is: Is a bibliographic record 'original'? Originality requires some intellectual input from the author. Most bibliographic records consist of a series of facts presented in a predetermined order according to AACR2 or other cataloguing codes of practice. In theory, everyone using these codes should produce exactly the same record. The fact that they do not is more to do with human fallibility than the rules themselves! It has been held that merely to follow exact instructions does not give the person actually doing the work any copyright in the work they create. For example, an architectural draughtsman following exact design instructions is not considered to have made a new copyright work. But it could be argued that human intellect had been used to implement the rules. Therefore it would be difficult to decide whether a catalogue record has any copyright as such, although the typography in a published catalogue would be protected (see paragraphs 4.88 and following).

4.7 **So are bibliographies not protected by copyright?**

Almost any bibliography will qualify as a database rather than a literary work and must be treated accordingly. The one exception is the scholarly bibliography, which may be annotated and is prepared by one identifiable person. See Section 9 for detailed information.

4.8 **Is a library catalogue protected?**

A library catalogue is almost certainly a database and will be protected as such under copyright law. See Section 9.

Dramatic works

4.9 **What is the difference between a literary and a dramatic work?**

A dramatic work is the non spoken part of a presentation and includes dance and mime. The words of a dramatic work are protected as a literary work. The term 'dramatic works' also covers choreography, dance and mime.

Example: A show like *West Side Story* will have separate copyrights in the words (literary work), the choreography and directions (dramatic work) and the music (musical work).

Musical works

4.10 Does 'musical work' mean anything with music included?

No. 'Musical work' means only the notes on the stave and excludes the words (which are a literary work) and any actions which go with the music, because they are dramatic works.

Example: *West Side Story* (as mentioned above in 'dramatic works') will have three separate copyrights: in the words; in the actions and movements of the dancers; and in the musical notes. Although this may sound complicated it is important, because the people who composed the three elements will each own a separate copyright which may expire at a different time. So the music may go out of copyright but not the words, or vice versa.

4.11 Does 'musical work' include a recording of the music?

No. That is separately covered as a sound recording (see Section 6).

4.12 What about a play performed and recorded on video?

The play is protected as a literary work and the video made of the performance is protected as a film, quite separately. The performers will also have separate rights in their performances.

Definition of author

It is important to define who the author of a work is, as this will usually determine how long copyright lasts. Copyright is most often linked to the death of the author. It is also important to note that the author is defined differently for different types of material, but for literary, dramatic and musical works the definitions are more or less the same.

4.13 What is the definition of 'the author'?

For literary, dramatic and musical works it is the person who created the work.

4.14   Does the author have to be a human person or can it be a company or organization?

The author must be a human being ('natural person' in legal terms). If no human author is identified the work is considered anonymous.

4.15   Supposing there are two or more authors?

They all count as the authors of the copyright.

4.16   Supposing it is not possible to find out who the author is?

A work is considered anonymous if the identity of the author cannot be traced by making reasonable enquiries.

4.17   What does 'reasonable enquiry' mean?

This is not defined but it would presumably require checking in major catalogues and relevant literary dictionaries, etc.

4.18   What happens if the author's identity is established later on?

Once the author's identity is established, then the work is no longer anonymous and the usual procedures apply.

4.19   Supposing the author has used a pseudonym?

Unless you can find out whose pseudonym it is, then the work is counted as anonymous. As with anonymous works, this would require reasonable enquiry, i.e. checking of literary reference works and major library catalogues. See paragraph 4.127 for an example.

4.20   What happens if a work definitely has more than one author, but not all their names are known?

Once the name of even one author is known, the work is no longer anonymous.

4.21   Supposing the author is given as an organization?

If no person is named as the author, the work is treated as anonymous.

4.22   If a work was generated by a computer, who counts as the author then?

The person who made the necessary arrangements for creating the work (but see Section 9).

4.23 **What about compilations such as directories, timetables, bibliographies and encyclopedias?**

If the work has a personal author, then that is the author. So a bibliography compiled by a named person is protected just as if it were a book. However, something like the *British National Bibliography* has no personal author, so is protected only as a database. Most works like this will qualify as databases (see Section 9), for which separate rules apply.

4.24 **What about works which have lots of articles by different people, such as an encyclopedia, which has articles signed by separate people?**

Then each article is protected as a separate work, and it may also be a database.

4.25 **Supposing some articles are signed and some not?**

They are all treated separately as individual works, so copyright in some will be treated as the work of an author and some will be anonymous.

Authors' rights

4.26 **Do authors of literary, dramatic and musical works all enjoy moral rights (as described in Section 3)?**

It depends on the type of material. Authors of monographs (books) and directors of films have the right to have the author's name included when the work is published. This right has to be asserted in writing. Authors of other works in this group do not have this right.

However, authors of works in this group do have the right to prevent derogatory treatment of their work (see paragraphs 3.4 and following).

4.27 **Who is the owner of copyright in a literary, dramatic or musical work?**

The basic rules are set out in Section 3 but there is a special additional exception for unpublished works. When an author leaves their unpublished manuscripts or other materials to a library, archive or museum as a bequest and their will does not specify any other arrangements then the presumption is that the copyright is also transferred to the library, archive or museum. They may specify differently in the will and, if they do, this will affect the way the unpublished material can be used.

Owners' rights

4.28   **What rights do owners of copyright in literary, dramatic and musical works have?**

Essentially copyright is a monopoly against which certain exceptions are set to make a balance between owner and user. This Section begins by looking at the rights which owners of copyright enjoy and then examining how they are limited by exceptions.

Copying

4.29   **Does the owner alone have the right to make copies?**

Yes, subject to the limitations mentioned later on.

4.30   **Does copying just mean photocopying?**

Certainly not. It means copying in any material form. This includes any method of copying, including, of course, resetting the type to make a new edition for publication, copying by hand or taking a photograph. Photocopying is clearly copying something and there are special provisions to allow some types of copying for some purposes. Copying also includes electronic copying, which includes storing a work in any form and copying the text onto a computer disc, converting it to electronically readable text using scanning equipment of various kinds, storing it on CD-ROM or transmitting it by fax. It also includes making copies of computer programs for any purpose.

4.31   **What else constitutes copying?**

Any action which uses the actual text that someone else has written, even if it is then changed. Of course, when someone takes a piece of another author's work and makes out that it is their own (plagiarism), then that is copying as well. The courts distinguish between actual copying and using someone else's ideas but not their actual text. So Dan Brown's famous work *The Da Vinci Code* was held to be based on the ideas in another book but did not actually copy the text.

4.32   **Using a computer, especially the internet, also involves copying. Is this not allowed either?**

The original 1988 Act gave the owner the exclusive right to control the making of copies which are transient or incidental to some other use of the work. So using the internet without permission would be an infringement! However, legislation passed in 2003 takes away the right of the owner to prevent you making these temporary copies. See paragraph 11.35 for more details.

4.33 **Fax involves copying. Is the use of fax really an infringement?**

Given that the law allows the making of temporary copies which have no independent significance, it would seem likely that merely sending a fax which produced nothing more than a paper copy at the other end would not be an infringement. However, if the process resulted in a stored electronic copy being generated and available for subsequent use, then this would probably be an infringement.

4.34 **Documents received by fax sometimes fade and disappear. Can the document be further copied as soon as it is received to make a durable copy?**

Not legally. Unlike the temporary copy made by a fax transmission, this is a permanent copy, so further copies should not be made. An exception might be a copy faxed for interlibrary loan (ILL) purposes, so the faxed copy might be further copied for preservation purposes.

4.35 **What about microforms?**

Making a microform is copying and is not permitted without the owner's consent. See paragraphs 4.253 and 5.4 for more detailed information.

4.36 **Can copies be made for committee meetings?**

No. Copying for committees is multiple copying and is not permitted unless the amount copied is less than substantial. However, in many organizations committee copying would be covered by an appropriate licence.

4.37 **Can a slide, overhead projector transparency or image for a PowerPoint presentation be made of a page of a book for teaching in a class or giving a lecture?**

Not under the law. The British Copyright Council has said that copying for a 'one off' lecture to, say, a local history group or for general classroom use would not be regarded by them as an infringement. Alternatively, if less than a substantial part were copied then it would be in order to make a slide of that part.

4.38   Some books and journals carry a warning that no part of the work can be reproduced, stored, etc. Does this take away the allowances given under the Copyright Act?

This statement has never been tested in law. It is generally thought unlikely that it would stand up in court, as it tries to prohibit what the law allows. There is an argument that it constitutes a contract between the publisher and the user about which the user knew perfectly well before buying the book, but general opinion is that it is there to frighten rather than to be enforced! Actual enforcement would be a very difficult thing to do and costly in legal fees to establish as binding. Of course, if it were binding, libraries could refuse to buy the books, which would make a considerable difference to publishers' sales. More recent books published by properly informed publishers preface this prohibitive statement with the phrase 'Except as permitted by the 1988 Copyright, Designs and Patents Act, . . .'

Issuing copies to the public

4.39   Is issuing copies to the public the same as publishing?

This is essentially what we would think of as traditional publishing, but note that the issue to the public does not have to be for money. Even if you distribute copies of someone's copyright work for free, it is still an infringement of their right to do this or to authorize others to do it.

4.40   If issuing copies to the public is an infringement, how can libraries offer a lending service?

The law makes it clear that the right to issue copies to the public only applies to works not previously made publicly available in the European Economic Area (EEA). So, once a work is published in the EEA it can be lent within the specific provisions for the lending and rental of copyright material (see 'lending and rental' under each type of material).

4.41   Does this idea of issuing copies to the public have any bearing on acquisition of materials by a library?

Essentially, no. If the work has been made legally available within the EEA then it can be legally acquired by a library, even if imported from another country. Any responsibility for infringing importation would rest with the bookseller involved, not the library. Libraries occasionally import single copies of a work but these are not for commercial purposes, so infringement is unlikely.

Performing rights

4.42 What are performing rights?

Every author has the right to decide if a work shall be performed in public, whether this is a recitation of a poem or of extracts from a book, or delivery of a speech. The author also has the right to decide whether the performance can be recorded. The performer has this last right too.

4.43 What about exhibiting a work. Does that count as performance?

Rather bizarrely, the answer is yes. So it would be an infringement to display a manuscript which was still in copyright to the general public in an exhibition.

4.44 Are performing rights really important for libraries and archives?

Libraries are increasingly involved in cultural activities and some have library theatres, so it is important to be aware of the owner's rights, especially when library materials may be used to put on performances. This includes plays, concerts and arts festivals generally. Increasingly, libraries and archives arrange poetry readings and also events in which stories are read to children.

4.45 Can only the copyright owner authorize performance?

Yes, although this may be done through a licensing agency (see Section 10).

4.46 Does performance mean just plays or presentations?

No. Performance includes delivery of speeches, lectures or sermons and also includes presentation by visual or audible means.

Example: If the library possesses some poems by a local author, they may not be copied. But it is also an infringement to recite them in public or make a video of someone reciting them in public. Family videos of weddings, for example, may infringe the copyright in the vicar's sermon if he is reading from a prepared text. However, if the vicar is speaking extempore, there is no copyright in the sermon until it has been recorded (on the video). The vicar then owns the copyright in the sermon and the person who recorded the video owns the copyright in the video as such!

4.47 Does this mean that poems cannot be used for public recitation?

Not quite. One person may read a reasonable extract from a copyright work in public, provided that the reading is accompanied by sufficient acknowledgement.

4.48 **What do the terms 'reasonable extract' and 'sufficient acknowledgement' mean?**

They are not defined. 'Reasonable extract' is a matter of judgement. 'Sufficient acknowledgement' would certainly mean saying who wrote the work, and when and where it was published, if published at all.

4.49 **What about story-telling for children in libraries?**

Technically this is an infringement by performance (see paragraphs 4.42 and following).

4.50 **Sometimes teachers want to perform plays or hold concerts using copyright library materials. Is this allowed?**

Yes, provided that only students, teachers and other persons directly connected with the educational establishment are present. This does not include mums and dads!

Communicating the work to the public by electronic means

4.51 **What exactly does this mean in practical terms?**

This right is defined as 'Communication to the public by electronic transmission', which includes:

• broadcasting the work
• making the work available by electronic transmission so that members of the public may access it from a place and at a time individually chosen by them.

This clearly includes putting material on a website, and therefore compensates for the previous definition of a broadcast, which specifically excluded websites and internet transmission.

See Section 8 for broadcasts.

4.52 **Supposing the broadcast also goes out on the internet at the same time?**

If the work is also transmitted via the internet at the same time as it is broadcast, or if the transmission is by internet only but at a time chosen solely by the person making the transmission (in other words using the internet as a broadcasting medium) then this is regarded as broadcasting and not as communicating the work to the public by electronic means. In a nutshell, broadcasting takes precedence over internet transmission when determining the status of a transmitted work.

4.53   Does this have any implications for libraries and archives?

As far as literary, dramatic or musical works go, the main fact to bear in mind is that broadcasting a work is an infringement of the owner's rights. So if a local radio station wished to use some of the library's holdings for broadcasting purposes, such as poems, musical compositions or extracts from local history material, this would not be allowed without permission. This would not apply if the use were solely for news reporting.

4.54   Does this have any effect on the use of websites?

Yes. The definition of this right makes it clear that putting anything on a website without the copyright owner's permission is an infringement.

Adaptation and translation

4.55   Does adaptation apply just to plays, novels or similar materials?

No. It includes translation, adaptation, conversion of dramatic works to non-dramatic works and turning a story into a cartoon or similar work. Translating a work is considered an adaptation and translations should not be made without due consideration of the purpose for which they are made and the use to which they will be put.

4.56   What can be done for a researcher in the laboratory of a company who needs a technical article translated?

As the use would be for a commercial purpose, the translation can be made only with the consent of the copyright owner.

4.57   What about a student who wants to translate a play from a foreign language?

If the student makes their own translation there is unlikely to be a problem as copying by non-mechanical means in the course of instruction is permitted (see paragraphs 4.166 and following). It would be interesting to test the exception if an automatic translating program were used!

4.58   **What is the position regarding religious texts?**

Any translation of a religious text will be protected by copyright. If it is the work of a specific translator, then the usual rules about how long copyright lasts will apply. If the translation is the work of a panel or group then it will be regarded as anonymous and the rules for anonymous works will apply. The original text from which the translation was made will probably be out of copyright anyway, unless it is very recent, so anyone can make their own translation and distribute it.

4.59   **Is it an infringement to rewrite a non-dramatic work as a dramatic one and vice versa?**

It is an infringement to rewrite a dramatic work as a non-dramatic one and vice versa. It is also an infringement to reproduce a story in another form, such as pictures.

Example: Someone decides to rework Alan Ayckbourn's *The Norman Conquests* as a novel. This is an infringement. Equally, it would be an infringement to produce a dramatic version of one of Catherine Cookson's novels.

4.60   **Does this restriction include turning a story into pictures, for example for a children's library?**

Yes. The law specifies that it is not allowed to turn the story into a version wholly or mainly told in the form of pictures suitable for reproduction in a book, newspaper or magazine. Although this is obviously aimed at the cartoon market, it has implications for children's libraries and school libraries as well.

4.61   **How does the rule on adaptation affect arrangements of musical works?**

Any arrangement of a transcription of a musical work counts as an adaptation. In one case the notation of a 17th-century musical work was changed so that it could be understood by modern musicians, although the actual music produced remained the same. This was considered an adaptation (and also a new work).

4.62   **Does 'translation' extend to computer 'languages'?**

Yes. The law specifically states that changing a program from one computer language to another is an infringement unless this is done incidentally during the running of the program. But see Section 11.

4.63   Supposing an adaptation or translation has been made quite legally. Does that also attract copyright?

Yes, and the person who made the adaptation has rights in the adaptation, just as the author has in the original work.

Lending and rental

4.64   Who is allowed to lend or rent copyright works to others?

Lending and rental are exclusive rights of the copyright owner but the rules governing them are quite complicated and many acts of lending are not considered as 'lending' for legal reasons.

4.65   What is actually meant by 'lending'?

The meaning of lending is defined in the legislation as follows:

- that a work is made available for use on the presumption that it will, or may be, returned
- the lending does not lead to any economic or commercial advantage to the lender
- the lending is done by an establishment which is accessible to the public OR by a prescribed library (see paragraphs 4.256 and following) which is not conducted for profit BUT by a public library only if the work is covered by the Public Lending Right Act or was acquired before 1 December 1996.

Lending does not include:

- making available for public performance
- performing in public
- broadcasting
- making available for exhibition purposes
- on-the-spot reference use
- making available between establishments accessible to the public.

4.66   Does this mean that a library which lends material cannot charge?

No. The necessary operating costs of the lending establishment may be recovered. Where lending takes place under these conditions it is not defined as 'lending'!

4.67   **What about organizations that are not accessible to the public?**

Lending undertaken by them is not within this legislation and is not therefore considered 'lending' in legal terms, even if it is in general terms.

4.68   **What does 'on-the-spot' mean?**

This is not defined but it would seem clear that use of a work within a library or similar collection where the work is not taken out of the room would be on-the-spot. Whether taking a work from one room in a building to another or from one building to another within a single site still constitutes on-the-spot is not clear. It seems unlikely that 'the spot' would be stretched to use on a different site.

4.69   **Which libraries can lend material?**

As educational establishments can lend any material, it would seem likely that the library of any such establishment could lend material to another library.

4.70   **What about other libraries?**

Any library which is a prescribed library (see paragraphs 4.256 and following) and which is not conducted for profit can lend material, so presumably it can be lent to other libraries.

4.71   **What about public libraries?**

As public libraries can lend only books within the Public Lending Right scheme, they can lend only these items to other libraries.

4.72   **What can public libraries lend?**

After 1 December 1996 public libraries can lend:

- any printed materials obtained before 1 December 1996
- only materials acquired after 1 December 1996 which are covered by the Public Lending Right Scheme or which would have been eligible for coverage by the scheme because of their form but are precluded because of country of origin, date of the author's death, or other similar reasons.

4.73   **What works would qualify under this last, rather confusing, definition?**

To try to clarify this, a new edition of a book by an author who died over 70 years ago is not eligible for PLR but would have been if the author had died recently.

To avoid the situation where the public library could not lend this book because it is outside the PLR scope, it can be treated for lending as if it is eligible, even though it is not!

4.74 What about books without authors, such as directories or bibliographies?

These can be for reference only, if acquired after 1 December 1996.

4.75 What about periodicals, maps or photographs?

If acquired after 1 December 1996, they must be for reference only.

4.76 What about lending works through interlibrary loan?

Care may be needed here. Lending between establishments which are accessible to the public is not counted as lending. BUT there are specific clauses dealing with libraries which will probably override this general exception, as normal practice is that where specific regulations exist they take precedence over general rules.

4.77 Can any library take part in these interlibrary loan arrangements?

It depends whether the library is being asked for copies or is asking for copies and whether the library wishes to lend or borrow.

4.78 Which libraries can lend to other libraries?

There is no legislation which deals directly with lending between libraries. 'Lending' is defined as not including 'making available between establishments which are accessible to the public' but (a) the term 'accessible to the public' is not defined and (b) there are separate clauses for lending from libraries which are not just establishments accessible to the public. However, some possible situations in which interlibrary loan can take place can be deduced.

4.79 What do these special arrangements permit?

These allow any prescribed library (see paragraph 4.256 and following for a definition of this term) which is not conducted for profit to lend copyright works. As lending is defined as not being for economic or commercial gain, the charging for this interlibrary lending should not cost more than the operating costs to carry out the lending. So a commercial or industrial library cannot lend, but it can borrow such items from other, non-profit prescribed libraries.

4.80   If a work has been borrowed by a library can it then be lent to an end-user?

It would seem that this will depend on whether that library can lend this type of material to end-users from its own collection. If lending from its own collection would not be allowed, it is unlikely that it could lend material from another collection which it could not lend from its own collection. For example, public libraries cannot lend issues of periodicals, so it would seem unlikely that a public library could borrow a back issue from another library (say, an educational library) and lend that to the end-user, when it cannot lend the same type of material from its own collection.

4.81   What about libraries in commerce and industry?

If the library is not accessible to the public, then what this library does is not considered lending for copyright purposes. However, if the library is accessible to the public, any library in this category cannot lend any material, but it may be able to borrow from other libraries. However, it would not be able to lend the material borrowed, as such libraries are not allowed to lend.

4.82   What about libraries in charities or other organizations?

If they are accessible to the public, then they are bound by the rules as set out above. If they are not accessible to the public, then presumably they can lend, as what they do is not considered lending from a copyright point of view.

4.83   What constitutes rental?

Rental is making something available for a limited time on the expectation that it will be returned and for which a charge above the necessary operating costs is recovered.

4.84   Can libraries have rental schemes?

Only with the agreement of the copyright owner.

Crown and Parliamentary copyright

4.85   What is Crown copyright?

When a work is created by an employee of the Crown it becomes subject to Crown copyright, which is technically owned by the Crown (Her Majesty), and different rules apply to this type of material.

4.86   Who counts as a Crown employee?

Since the distancing of much civil service work from central government and recent moves to devolution this is no longer clear. Major government departments and ministries are Crown but the status of many bodies (for example the British Library and national museums) is that they are not Crown even if owned and funded by the government. A full list of which organizations are and are not Crown can be found on the Office of Public Sector Information website (see Appendix 2 for details).

4.87   What is Parliamentary copyright?

Parliamentary copyright exists in any work commissioned by either or both Houses of Parliament.

Typographical arrangements of published editions

4.88   What is typographical copyright?

Every published work has two copyrights: one in the actual content of the text and the other in the printed layout of the page.

4.89   What is the point of these two copyrights?

It means that if a publisher publishes or republishes a work that is out of copyright, such as Shakespeare's plays, they still have some protection for their efforts in setting up the typography and producing the book, even though the actual content can be freely published by someone else.

4.90   Who counts as the author of the typographical arrangement of a work?

The publisher.

Publication right

4.91   What is publication right?

Publication right is a right introduced on 1 December 1996. It is similar to, but distinct from, copyright as such.

4.92   Does publication right exist in all works?

No, but it can exist in any literary, dramatic, musical or artistic work or a film.

4.93 ## So when does it exist?

Publication right exists when anyone in the EEA first publishes a work which

- is out of copyright
- is published by someone who is an EEA citizen
- has not been previously published in the UK or any EEA state.

For a definition of the EEA see 4.102.

4.94 ## Does 'published' mean published commercially?

No. In the context of publication right (and the definition is different in different contexts) it means:

- communication to the public (an undefined term) and in particular:
- issue of copies to the public
- making the work available by means of an electronic retrieval system
- rental or lending of copies to the public
- performance, showing or exhibiting in public
- broadcasting.

4.95 ## When does an unpublished work go out of copyright?

See paragraphs 4.110 and following for details but note that unpublished literary, dramatic and musical works the author of which had died before 1 January 1969 are protected for 50 years from the date when the new law came into force (i.e. 1989) and therefore do not come out of copyright until 31 December 2039, the first date on which publication right for these classes of works can come into force. Unpublished works the author of which died after 31 December 1968 enjoy the usual 70 years' protection unless the author is a national of a non-EEA country, in which case copyright lasts for as long as that country provides protection.

4.96 ## Does this mean that, where publication right comes into force, libraries and archives lose control of unpublished material in their collections?

Fortunately, no. The publication can take place only with the consent of the owner of the physical material in which the work is recorded. So a library or archive could refuse to allow a work to be published or permit it only under strict conditions (including royalties!).

4.97 **Are there any works which may be subject to publication right now?**

No, not until 31 December 2039.

Making available right (see Sections 11.47–48)

4.98 **Does making available right apply to literary, dramatic and musical works?**

No, only to the performances of them.

Duration of copyright in literary, dramatic and musical works

4.99 **Does copyright last for the same period for all literary, dramatic and musical works?**

No. There are different periods of copyright as described below.

Published works

4.100 **What constitutes 'published'?**

'Published' means issuing copies to the public. This in turn means putting into circulation copies not previously put into circulation. Note that the emphasis is on copies. Making a single copy does not of itself constitute publication. The definition also includes making the work available through an electronic retrieval system.

4.101 **How long does copyright last for published literary, dramatic and musical works?**

This depends on the country of origin of the work. If the work was published in an EEA country (see the next paragraph for a definition of the EEA), or the author is an EEA national, then the copyright in published literary, dramatic or musical works lasts for 70 years from the end of the calendar year in which the author dies. Copyright always expires on 31 December, never in the middle of a year.

Example: Author died on 5 January 1942. Copyright expires on 31 December 2011. Author died on 29 December 1942. Copyright still expires on 31 December 2011.

4.102 **What is the EEA?**

The European Economic Area which comprises (as at April 2009) Austria, Belgium, Bulgaria, Cyprus, the Czech Republic, Denmark, Estonia, Finland, France, Germany, Greece, Hungary, Iceland, Ireland, Italy, Latvia, Liechtenstein, Lithuania, Luxembourg, Malta, the Netherlands, Norway, Poland, Portugal, Romania, Slovakia, Slovenia, Spain, Sweden and the United Kingdom.

4.103 **What about works published outside the EEA?**

These are protected for the same length of time as they would be in their own country if none of the authors is an EEA national. If a work is published in a country which gives only 50 years' protection, then that is all it will get within the EEA.

4.104 **Supposing it was published simultaneously in several countries both within and outside the EEA?**

In this case, it is considered as an EEA publication. Note that 'simultaneous' means within 30 days of first publication. So a work could be published in, say, Australia on one day but, provided it was also published in an EEA country within 30 days of that first publication, it would still qualify for EEA protection.

4.105 **Supposing the work is anonymous or has no personal author?**

Anonymous works first published within the EEA, which include works which have no personal author, such as annual reports of organizations, or anything with no identifiable personal author, remain in copyright for 70 years from the end of the year in which they are created. If they are published during that period, then the 70-year period starts all over again. Otherwise the work is protected for the length of time it would have been protected in the country of origin (usually 50 years).

4.106 **Supposing the author died before the work was published, does this make a difference?**

If the work was published after the author died, but before 1 January 1969, then copyright expires 50 years from the end of the year in which the work was published. If the author died on or after 1 January 1969, then the 70-year rule applies as in other cases (but see paragraph 4.103 for non-EEA authors).

Compilations and periodicals

4.107 **What about works made up of contributions by several people?**

The copyright expires separately for each contribution. So the copyrights in papers in a conference proceedings all expire at different times, depending when each contributor dies. However, the copyright in the typography will expire 25 years after the end of the year of publication (see paragraphs 4.88 on typographical arrangement).

4.108 **When does the copyright in a periodical issue run out?**

The copyright in each article will run out 70 years after the death of the author (as for any other published literary work), but the copyright in the periodical issue as a whole (i.e. the typography) will expire 25 years after publication. If the periodical was published outside the EEA and none of the authors is an EEA national, then copyright lasts for only as long as the country of publication provides.

4.109 **Supposing the work contains illustrations by someone other than the author?**

The copyrights in the text and in the illustrations are quite separate.

Example: The text of the Pooh Bear stories was written by A. A. Milne, who died in 1956 (copyright expires 2026), but the illustrations were drawn by E. H. Shepard, who died in 1976 (copyright expires 2046).

Unpublished works

4.110 **What if the work is unpublished?**

The situation may sound complicated. If the author died before 1 January 1969, was a national of an EEA state and the work was unpublished at that time, copyright expires on 31 December 2039. If the author died on or after 1 January 1969, the work is protected for 70 years from the end of the year in which the author dies. If the author is not a national of an EEA state, then copyright expires at the end of the term of protection which the author's national laws give.

Example: Author died 22 November 1955. Copyright expires 31 December 2039. Author dies 3 December 1990. Copyright expires 31 December 2060 (death + 70 years).

4.111 **What if the author is still alive?**

Copyright will last until 70 years after the end of the year in which the author dies, just as for a published work; or, if the author is from outside the EEA, the length of time that the author's own country gives.

4.112   Does this mean that all unpublished works cannot be used by anyone until 2039?

No. If the work was held by the library, museum or archive before 1 August 1989 and the author was already dead, then these documents can be copied, even with a view to publication, provided that the author has been dead for 50 years if the document is 100 years old or more. Note that copying is allowed 'with a view to publication' – the library or archive does not authorize publication: clearance for this must be arranged by the prospective publisher.

Example: Author wrote a poem in 1875 and died in 1910. The poem could be copied after 31 December 1975. Note, however, that 'view to publication' does not mean it can be published – only copied in preparation for plans to seek permission to publish.

4.113   What about anonymous/pseudonymous works?

Unpublished anonymous or pseudonymous works are protected for 70 years from the end of the year in which they are created, or 70 years from first being made available to the public. However, where a work was created before 1 August 1989 copyright protection must last until 2039 regardless of the assumed date of creation. Despite this, if it is reasonable to assume that the author has been dead for 70 years, then the work can be treated as out of copyright.

4.114   What happens once anonymous/pseudonymous works are published?

They are protected for 70 years from the end of the year in which they were published. This includes not only publishing, but also public performance or broadcasting.

4.115   Supposing it is not possible to judge when a document was created?

There are special provisions for this situation. Where it is not possible by reasonable enquiry to find the identity of the author, and it is reasonable to suppose the copyright has expired, then the work may be treated as out of copyright.

4.116   What constitutes 'reasonable'?

This is not defined. Common sense and professional judgement are needed to make a guesstimate as to when a work might have been written. One learned judge said that 'what is reasonable is what seems reasonable to the man on the Clapham omnibus'.

4.117   How is the length of copyright worked out if there are several authors?

Where a work has joint authorship, copyright lasts until 70 years after the end of the year in which the last author dies. If at least one of the authors is known, then any unknown ones are disregarded. Where some authors are EEA nationals and others are not, the work is treated as qualifying for the EEA term of protection (death + 70 years), or death of the last author to die if this gives a longer term of protection.

Example: A work has three authors – two are EEA nationals and one is not. The two EEA nationals die in 1955 and 1960 respectively, giving a term of protection until 2030, but the third, non-EEA author, whose country gives 50 years' protection, does not die until 1995, giving protection until 2045.

Crown and Parliamentary copyright

4.118   How long does Crown copyright last?

Crown copyright in a literary, dramatic or musical work lasts for 125 years from the year in which the work was created or 50 years from the year in which it was first commercially published, provided this happens within 75 years of the year of creation. In other words, 125 years is the maximum.

Example: A report is prepared in 1930. Its copyright will run out in 2055. But if it is published commercially, say, in 1960, then the copyright runs out in 2010.

4.119   What if the author in the example did not die until 1970?

It makes no difference. Length of Crown copyright is linked to date of creation or date of publication, not the human being responsible for creating the work.

4.120   Supposing some papers were not released because of the 'Thirty Year Rule' and were secret until then?

This makes no difference. Copyright runs from the year in which the work was created.

4.121   How long does Parliamentary copyright last?

It lasts for 50 years from the year in which the work was created.

4.122   Are the publications of other governments protected in the same way?

No. Publications of other governments are protected as if they were ordinary commercial publications in the UK. In the case of the USA, the US Government claims no copyright in its own publications within the USA and it would seem unlikely that they should be protected in the UK in a way that they are not in the USA. So it is generally assumed that USGPO (United States Government Printing Office) publications are not protected by copyright.

Typographical copyright

4.123   How long does typographical copyright last?

Typographical copyright lasts for 25 years from the end of the year in which the work is published.

4.124   So when does the copyright in a published work actually expire?

There are two dates. One, usually the earlier, will be the typographical one, which is 25 years after first publication. However, the author's copyright continues until 70 (or 50) years after death. So the copyright in a book runs out in two stages. This does nothing to help people who want to copy it within that 25-year period, of course. However, it does allow republication by another publisher if the author has retained the copyright and not assigned it exclusively to the first publisher.

4.125   Does this mean that every time a book is reprinted the copyright begins again?

No. If the reprint is simply a reproduction of the original typographical arrangement, no new copyright comes into force.

4.126   Supposing it is a new layout of the book?

Then typographical copyright subsists in that particular edition.

4.127   What if it is the same typesetting but a long new introduction has been written?

There will be a new copyright in the new introduction, owned originally by the author of that introduction. The publisher can claim copyright in the whole work (introduction and text together) but the original text will only be a reproduction of an earlier text and is covered only for the time that typographical copyright lasts.

Example: The Best of Saki, introduction by Tom Sharpe. London, Pan Books, 10th impression 1983. First published 1976.

Initially it looks anonymous, but Saki is the pen name of Hector Hugo Munro, killed in action in 1916. Copyright in the stories expired in 1966 (author's death + 50 years as the rule was then). The publisher published them in 1976, so no permission was needed as the stories were out of copyright. Typography was set up in 1976, so copyright in that expired in 2001 (25 years). The 10th impression in 1983 is not new typography so no new copyright exists. However, the introduction is by Tom Sharpe, who is still very much alive, so only that element of the book is still in copyright.

Copying materials

4.128   Can any copying at all be carried out without permission?

The law makes certain exceptions to the exclusive rights which owners enjoy over their works. The most important for libraries, archives and information providers are certain rights to copy and lend copyright works.

4.129   For what purposes can a copyright work be used without the owner's consent?

There are several reasons given in the law. The most commonly claimed and most frequently quoted is fair dealing.

Exceptions
Fair dealing

4.130   What is fair dealing?

Fair dealing is a concept which has never been defined. What it seems to say is that there may be good reasons for using something so long as the use does not harm the copyright owner or author but nevertheless benefits either the individual or society generally.

4.131 Does fair dealing just mean copying a work?

No. It includes copying but also using material in presentations, broadcasts, films and websites.

4.132 Does fair dealing apply to all copyright works?

Yes, but the different types of fair dealing apply differently to different classes of material. This section deals with literary, dramatic and musical works. For other works see the relevant chapters. It applies to literary, dramatic and musical works for non-commercial research and private study and also for news reporting and criticism and review.

4.133 How much of a work can be copied under fair dealing?

Nobody knows for certain – it is a matter of individual judgement in each case. What is clear is that until a substantial part of a work is copied, there can be no infringement, so such defences as fair dealing are not needed.

4.134 Does copying just mean photocopying?

No. The copying can be done using any methods, as the law does not specify the method of copying. See paragraph 4.30. So it also includes using a digital camera or mobile phone.

4.135 What is a substantial part?

See paragraphs 3.35–36.

4.136 So is there no guidance at all as to what fair dealing actually is?

In the law, no. Various guidelines have been issued in the past but they are guidelines only.

4.137 How can anyone judge if copying something is 'fair'?

Look at the amount to be copied in conjunction with the reason for making the copy. No concrete examples can be given, but consider the following: Copying a whole work, which has long been out of print and unavailable, might be 'fair' but copying the same work just to save buying a copy is obviously not. It must be emphasized that research must be for a non-commercial purpose.

4.138 What are the justifications for fair dealing?

The law recognizes several. The one most commonly cited in libraries is copying for non-commercial research or private study. The other purposes are criticism and review and reporting current events.

Research for a non-commercial purpose

4.139 What constitutes 'research'?

The word is not defined in law but the court would probably give it its natural meaning.

4.140 What does 'non-commercial' mean?

The law does not say and it must be up to each individual to decide if the copying is (a) fair and (b) for a non-commercial purpose. The Intellectual Property Office has some general guidance on its website (www.ipo.gov.uk) but this is not legally binding.

4.141 Are there any other restrictions?

Yes. When copying something for non-commercial research purposes the source must be acknowledged.

4.142 What can be done for someone who does want a copy for commercial purposes?

The copying must be carried out with the permission of the copyright owner. Usually this is done through a licence offered by the appropriate licensing agency (see Section 10), but if none of the licences mentioned there applies, then permission must be sought directly from the copyright owner. This may be the author or the publisher, depending on the circumstances.

4.143 Is private study limited to students?

Not at all, if by 'student' is meant someone in an academic institution. Anyone undertaking training or education of any kind, including leisure courses such as evening classes in hobbies or holiday languages, can reasonably claim fair dealing as a 'student'. But to do this the copying must be done by the STUDENT personally and not on behalf of the student.

4.144 Can this be done by someone in industry and commerce?

This would be difficult to justify, as the definition of private study now specifically excludes 'any study which is directly or indirectly for a commercial purpose'. So, once again, the user will need to make this judgement for each copy made for private study purposes.

4.145 Why private study?

Private study is thought of as being done alone. Therefore multiple copying for classroom use cannot be for private study and is provided for separately under educational copying (see below).

4.146 Does fair dealing allow the making of more than one copy?

If the student or researcher does the copying themselves it might be possible to make more than one copy.

Example: Suppose a student has to go on a geography field trip. Two copies of a small portion of a map may be needed, one for use in the field (where it may get muddy or torn) and the other for the file relating to the project. If two copies are made they must be for the personal use only of the person who made them. But this is merely an opinion.

4.147 Supposing the student wants a copy for personal use and one for a friend?

Not allowed! If any copying is done on behalf of someone else, the person making the copy must not make it if they know that this will result in a copy of substantially the same material being supplied to more than one person at substantially the same time and for substantially the same purpose. But always remember that your institution may have a licence, which would allow this.

Example: Three students may make for themselves one copy each of, say, a journal article, for use in a lecture or project. But if one makes copies for personal use and copies for the two friends, then this is an infringement.

4.148 What do all these 'substantially's mean?

They are not defined but it would seem likely that someone copying pages 9–14 for themselves and pages 10–16 for a friend or colleague would have copied 'substantially the same material' and that this copying, if done on Monday and Wednesday of the same week for use in the same tutorial or related experiments at the laboratory bench, would constitute 'at substantially the same time' and 'for substantially the same purpose'.

4.149 What about self-service machines then?

Although these are not dealt with specifically, the Act differentiates between copies made by students/researchers themselves and those made for them by other people. Although nothing is said in this context about providing equipment which might be used for infringing purposes, it is clear from another part of the Act that it is not an offence to possess equipment which can be used for breach of copyright, as opposed to equipment which can be used only for breach of copyright. It would be foolish of any librarian deliberately to turn a blind eye to copying which was beyond the law, and a suitable notice giving details of what is and is not allowed should be displayed (contact CILIP for a suggested text), but whether a librarian could actually be held responsible is open to doubt. Any notice should refer to the CDPA and its restrictions. These should also be mentioned in any publicity for the library's services and any user-education courses which are offered. Generally, librarians are expected to use their best endeavours to ensure that machines in their care are not used for infringements of copyright.

4.150 What if the person asks the librarian to do the copying for them?

What the law says, in a rather roundabout way, is that copying by libraries is only fair dealing if the special conditions about copying by libraries are observed. If the library steps outside these conditions, then the copying is not fair dealing and becomes an infringement. Copying by libraries is dealt with in detail in paragraphs 4.182 and following.

4.151 What about downloading from databases?

See Section 9 on databases for detailed guidance.

4.152 What about databases stored on CD-ROM?

See Section 9 on databases.

Criticism or review

4.153 Can libraries claim that they use material for criticism or review?

An important one for librarians of all kinds is criticism or review. It is allowed to quote parts of a work when writing critical essays or reviews such as book reviews or comparisons of different authors' works in academic research.

4.154   How much can be quoted?

That is open to individual judgement, but you must not quote so much that it saves the reader from having to consult/buy the original. The source of the quotations must be given, e.g. the full bibliographic reference in a review is essential, as the reviewer may be encouraging the reader to buy a copy! The same is true if a criticism is being written of the writings of a single author. Libraries which prepare their own reviews for the general public or in the form of information bulletins for researchers should note the conditions under which, and to what extent, they can quote the works mentioned.

4.155   Are there any rules to be observed?

Yes. The work quoted must have been made available to the public and the source of the quotation must be acknowledged.

4.156   What does 'made available to the public' mean?

In this context it includes:

- the issue of copies to the public
- making the work available by means of an electronic retrieval system
- rental or lending of copies of the work to the public
- performance, exhibition, playing or showing of the work in public
- communication of the work to the public.

4.157   Does this review idea extend to news bulletins?

No. See the following paragraphs.

Reporting current events

4.158   What is a current event?

A current event is something defined less by time than by current interest. It can be something which happened yesterday or today, but equally, it might be something that happened several years ago but which has a bearing on events happening now.

4.159   Can any material be used?

Any work can be used except a photograph.

4.160 Supposing the news items that are needed include a photograph?

Clearly, the law is intended to protect the very considerable investment in photography made by newspapers and without this exception any evening paper could use the photographs of any morning one for its news story. In theory this applies to internal and local news bulletins made from clippings but it is very difficult to exclude a photograph in the middle of a piece of news text. Technically it should be blacked out. The alternative is to retype the necessary text. But see Section 10 for possible copying under licence from the Newspaper Licensing Agency.

4.161 Supposing the news bulletin is prepared and displayed electronically?

The same rules apply as for a clippings service.

4.162 Are there any other restrictions?

Yes, the source of the work quoted must be acknowledged, unless this is not possible for reasons of practicality or otherwise.

4.163 What does that mean?

Presumably, it means you must acknowledge the source if you can find it out.

Educational copying

See also Section 10 on licences.

4.164 Are the amounts which may be copied for educational copying just as vague as in fair dealing?

No, the rules are quite different.

4.165 What is the difference between copying for educational purposes and copying for private study?

Private study does not mean for classroom use. Educational copying can be for classroom use. All librarians in any organization where teaching takes place should be aware of what is allowed, as the materials in their care are frequently used for educational purposes. This is also true for public libraries, which are used for project work. Educational copying exceptions do not apply to training in commercial/industrial companies.

4.166 Can a teacher or student copy anything for use in the classroom?

A teacher or student may copy out all or part of a copyright work in the course of instruction (e.g. a poem) onto the blackboard or into an exercise book for the purposes of instruction, but they may not copy it using a reprographic process, i.e. not by photocopying or scanning it.

4.167 Does instruction apply only to schools and universities?

No, but the instruction must be for a non-commercial purpose. So training/education in a commercial company is excluded but purely internal training in, say, a military organization, may well be included.

4.168 Can any amount be copied?

If the work is unpublished, then any amount may be copied. If it has been made available to the public, then the copying must be fair. In other words, so much of a work must not be copied that it becomes unnecessary to buy a copy or copies of the work for teaching purposes, or that it avoids the need to make copies under the CLA licence.

4.169 What does 'made available to the public' mean?

It has the same definition as for criticism and review. See paragraph 4.156.

4.170 Are there any other restrictions?

Yes, the source of the work must be acknowledged.

4.171 What about copying for examinations?

Anything can be copied for the purposes of setting the questions or providing the answers except sheet music, which may not be photocopied to enable the student to perform the work. A further problem is determining when continuously assessed work counts as part of an examination and when it is classroom teaching.

4.172 Does 'anything' really mean anything?

Yes, except for musical scores as mentioned above.

4.173 What if a student needs to include some copyright material in a thesis for a degree?

This would seem to be covered in providing the answers to an examination. If the thesis is subsequently copied for other purposes or published, then clearance would be needed from the copyright owner.

4.174   What happens if several children come into the public library, all asking for copies of the same thing for their project?

Only one copy can be provided. It is unclear at what age a child could sign the necessary form (see paragraph 4.209) as a legal minor. However, although schools operated by local authorities usually have a licence to copy necessary materials, such licences may allow copying only from books and magazines in the school's own collection and not those held by other libraries. Teachers should check with the CLA or NLA terms as appropriate.

4.175   Are there any restrictions?

Yes, the source of the material quoted in examination questions must be acknowledged, but students do not have to acknowledge the source when answering them. But it would be a poor answer that contained unacknowledged quotes!

4.176   What about including some copyright material in collections put together by teachers?

There are special rules governing this which should be known by the teacher or publisher and will not concern the librarian too much. Section 33 of the Act sets out the limits for this sort of publishing, for which librarians are sometimes asked to provide the original material to copy.

4.177   What about using material in VLEs?

See paragraph 11.53.

Copying for educational establishments
4.178   What counts as an educational establishment?

An educational establishment is defined as:

- any school
- any university allowed to award degrees under Act of Parliament or Royal Charter
- any institution empowered to offer further or higher education under the Education (Scotland) Act, 1980, the Education and Libraries (Northern

Ireland) Order 1986 or the Education Reform Act (1988) (see SI 2005/223 for exact details)

- any theological college.

4.179 Can anyone else exercise these privileges?

Yes, any organization, provided that the education is for a non-commercial purpose.

4.180 Multiple copying is not allowed and fair dealing does not extend to classroom copying, so what can be done for teachers who need multiple copies of parts of works for use in instruction? Surely they do not have to rely on writing everything out by hand?

No! The Act allows one of two ways forward. If a licence is obtainable to cover the needed materials, then that licence should be taken out and adhered to. All local authorities and many universities have taken out such a licence and the first thing is to check what it covers and what it allows. If no licence is obtainable, then the law allows that up to 1% of a work may be copied for classroom use in any three-month period specified by the Act. (The Act actually lays down that these periods are fixed as 1 January to 31 March, 1 April to 30 June, 1 July to 30 September and 1 October to 31 December.) These allowances may not be claimed if the person doing the copying knew, or ought to have known, that a licensing scheme was available, but no licensing scheme is allowed to restrict copying to less than the 1% allowed by law.

4.181 Can the library do this copying on behalf of the teacher/lecturer?

Yes. But make sure that the terms of the licence are known before agreeing to do such copying.

Libraries and archives

4.182 Are there exceptions for libraries and archives?

These exceptions are the most important limitation on owner's rights, as far as librarians and archivists are concerned. The main user group mentioned in the Act is libraries and archives. The special exceptions for libraries and archives apply to literary, dramatic and musical works but not to artistic works. There are no special exceptions for museums (other than copying unpublished works, see paragraphs

4.112 and following). These exceptions are often referred to as 'library privilege'. This is a useful shorthand term but is not a legal one. Note that the rules governing these exceptions apply where the librarian or archivist makes the copies on behalf of the user. Where users copy for themselves, they claim fair dealing and not library privilege.

4.183   Are the terms 'library' and 'archive' defined?

No. There are definitions of prescribed libraries and archives but not of libraries and archives generally.

4.184   Are the terms interchangeable?

No. Specific allowances are given to libraries and archives separately.

Copying published literary, dramatic and musical works

4.185   So what are libraries allowed to do that is special?

Quite a lot. First, they can supply copies of works to their users.

Copying for users – periodicals

4.186   What constitutes a periodical?

This is not defined. The word 'periodical' implies some concept of being issued at periods of time. Therefore monographs in series, technical report literature and publishers' series would probably not count as periodicals, as they are not linked to any timescale. A further problem could be newspapers. Although most librarians view newspapers as periodicals some dictionaries define the word 'periodical' as excluding newspapers!

4.187   Is there a limit on how much of a work can be copied for a user?

Yes. There are different limits for different kinds of material. In the case of a periodical, no user can be supplied with a copy of more than one article from the same periodical issue.

4.188   Can the user have more than one copy of the same article?

Not under the law. This must be done with the permission of the copyright owner. See Section 10 on licences.

4.189 **Supposing the volume of separate issues has been bound, how does this affect copying?**

The law is not specific but it seems likely that the interpretation would be that not more than one article could be copied from any one original periodical part as issued to the public.

4.190 **Supposing the article includes some drawings or photographs. Is it allowed to copy these as well?**

Yes. If an article is copied for someone, then it is allowed to copy any accompanying illustrations. Accompanying is an important word. If the article is in, say, an art journal and is supplemented by high-quality plates of paintings just to further illustrate the artist's work, these may not be copied unless they are intrinsic to the understanding of the text.

4.191 **What counts as an 'article'?**

Unfortunately this term is defined only in very general terms. An article, in the context of an article in a periodical, means an item of any description.

4.192 **Does this include things like advertisements, the title page, contents page or index?**

Yes, so the user should not really be supplied with an article from an issue and also the contents page.

4.193 **What about making copies of contents pages and circulating them for information among staff?**

This is not allowed. In the first place, it is multiple copying and second, the library cannot make copies for people unless they sign the declaration form first. However, as the contents page is a statement of a series of facts (which are not in themselves covered by copyright) there seems no reason why the contents page cannot be retyped, avoiding copying the typographical arrangement.

4.194 **So is copying title pages not allowed at all?**

It would be possible to circulate one copy of the contents page among staff, provided one of them asked for the copy in the first place. Alternatively, it is a good idea to write to the publishers concerned and ask if they will permit this. Most say they will, as it is good advertising for their journals, but some take the view that it could encourage related copying (i.e. more than one copy requested by different people at the same time for the same purpose).

4.195 Supposing the user wants two articles from the same issue?

Only one can be provided. However, it might be possible for the user to claim fair dealing if the user borrowed the periodical issue and made the copies personally. This would then require a fair dealing defence (see paragraphs 4.130 onwards). An alternative would be to copy under a licence.

4.196 If a publisher charges a higher rate for a library subscription to a periodical, can more copying be done?

No, unless the publisher has specifically stated this in the publicity, catalogues or in a specific letter to the library.

4.197 Can articles be copied from newspapers?

Yes. Whether the rules for copying from monographs or periodicals apply is slightly doubtful. Note also that there is a Newspaper Licensing Agency (see Section 10 on licences).

4.198 But to copy one article from a newspaper often involves incidentally copying another, or at least part of another. What is the position then?

Technically only the article actually required can be copied. To be perfectly correct all other parts of the page should be blanked out! But this would really be incidental copying, as an accident or done simply in the normal process of doing what is allowed. If a case were brought, it might be possible to argue, by analogy, incidental copying similar to that allowed for artistic works in photographs (see paragraph 5.25) but that is only an opinion.

4.199 Does the copying of articles extend to conference proceedings?

It will depend on the nature of the conference publication. Many annual or more frequent conferences appear simply as 'Proceedings of the xth conference on . . .' and could be viewed as a serial. Others with no clear numbering, or with monographic titles, must be treated as books. If the conference is held regularly, then it could be a periodical (annual is the most common). Conferences which are merely numbered, with no indication of the timescale in which they are held, will most likely be monographs (non-periodical publications).

4.200   What about technical reports in a numbered series?

Generally these must be treated as separate monographs.

4.201   Supposing the periodical issue consists of just one article?

The law specifically states that one article may be copied from a periodical issue. It seems clear that this allows the copying of an article if it constitutes the entire issue of a periodical although any other material in that issue, such as title page, advertisements or other ephemeral material must not be copied.

4.202   What about individually tailored information services?

The arrangement whereby the librarian scans various information services for material that is considered relevant to the research of library users and then obtains copies of these items and passes them on to users without being asked for them is an infringement.

4.203   What can be done for researchers in this situation?

There is no reason why a librarian may not produce a current awareness bulletin from which staff select and request items they require, but they must ask for items and not have them sent gratuitously. See paragraph 4.158 on current awareness bulletins.

Copying for users – monographs

4.204   Are there restrictions on copying from monographs?

The law does not use the word 'monograph' (or 'book' except in relation to Public Lending Right) but rather 'published edition other than an article in a periodical'.

4.205   What about books (monographs)?

The librarian may supply one copy of not more than a reasonable proportion of a book to a reader.

4.206   What constitutes a 'reasonable' proportion?

This is not defined, but a general view from the publishing industry has been that '10% or a chapter' might be reasonable. Although this is not a legal definition it is a helpful guideline. It seems safe to assume that a reasonable proportion is larger than a substantial part, because if less than a substantial part had been copied, there would be no need to claim any defence. Like substantial part and fair dealing, this is a matter of individual judgement.

4.207 Supposing a book consists mostly of photographs and plates?

Each item will be a copyright item in its own right and must be treated as such. Libraries may not copy artistic works (such as photographs and plates) on behalf of users unless they accompany the text requested. So the library may copy illustrations which accompany text but not items that are primarily illustrations with just a few words of text as, say, a caption.

Restrictions on copying for users

4.208 Can any librarian copy for someone under these conditions?

Yes. But the copying must be for research for a non-commercial purpose. This is likely to exclude copying by librarians in any commercial or industrial context.

4.209 Are there other restrictions?

Yes. The librarian can copy an article from a periodical or part of a published work only if the user signs a declaration form which states:

- that a copy has not previously been supplied
- that the copy will not be used except for research for a non-commercial purpose or private study and that a copy will not be supplied to any other person
- that to the best of [his] knowledge no person with whom [he] works or studies has made or intends to make at about the same time a request for substantially the same material for substantially the same purpose
- that if the declaration is false the copy becomes an infringing copy and the reader is responsible as if [he] had made the copy [him]self.

In addition, the user is required to pay a sum which will not only cover the cost of making the copy but make a general contribution towards the running of the library.

4.210 **Those 'substantiallys' have turned up again. Are they defined in this part of the Act any better than in the other?**

In a word, no. The same uncertainty applies (see paragraphs 3.35–36).

4.211 **Can a user really be expected to sign a statement about the intentions of other people?**

No, that is not what is being asked. Users sign to say that to the best of their knowledge nobody else is going to ask for copies of substantially the same material. . . . Thus the user can be in complete ignorance and truthfully sign the form.

4.212 **Does this declaration have to be made when the request is made?**

No. But it must be made before the copy is handed over. These two actions often coincide in smaller libraries but in large libraries or public libraries there is often a waiting time between the request and the arrival of the copy. It is perfectly in order to obtain the signed declaration at the time the request is made but it must be borne in mind that in some circumstances a copy may not be supplied, but the original lent instead. In this case the declaration is superfluous. On the other hand, the requester may not be aware that the request will be fulfilled by a photocopy, so it would be reasonable not to ask for a signature until the document was handed over.

4.213 **What happens when requests are received by telephone or letter?**

It may be possible that the request can be processed, but the copies cannot be handed over until the declaration form has been signed. This may well cause rather long correspondence but there is no easy way round this.

4.214 **Can the declaration be sent by fax?**

It seems likely. Fax is widely regarded in legal circles as an adequate substitute for the actual signed document. Much larger transactions than library photocopies are settled in this way!

4.215 **Can the declaration be made electronically rather than by visiting the library in person?**

Although the Electronic Communications Act allows electronic signatures for all kinds of transactions, in relation to cases where legislation specifically requires a physical signature, this must be repealed. As at February 2009 this has not happened for this provision in copyright law.

4.216 Must payment be made before the copies are handed over?

No, but payment must be made at some point. (See paragraph 4.242 onwards.)

4.217 What if the person making the request lives overseas?

This makes no difference. Even though the amounts may be small, payment cannot be avoided.

4.218 What if something is required urgently?

You need to use ingenuity, but the law must be observed.

4.219 Is there a standard form in which the declaration must be made?

Yes. The text is published in Statutory Instrument 89/1212 Schedule 2 Form A (as amended in 2003) and also in Appendix 3 at the end of this book.

4.220 So, as long as these conditions are met, can any librarian copy for a user?

It is not so simple. The user must sign a declaration but, in addition, the librarian must be satisfied that the requirements of two or more people are not

- similar
- related

and that no person is furnished with

- more than one copy
- more than one article from a periodical issue or more than a reasonable part of any other published work.

4.221 How can a librarian tell if the requirements of two or more users are 'similar'?

'Similar' is defined only in terms of substantially the same material at substantially the same time and for substantially the same purpose!

4.222 **So is there really no guidance as to what these terms mean?**

No. It is fairly easy to give examples of what would be regarded as substantial, as in paragraph 4.148, but it is very difficult to say what would not be regarded as substantial in these terms.

4.223 **How can a librarian tell if requirements are related?**

This is a lot easier. Related is defined as 'those persons receive instruction to which material is relevant at the same time and place'. This is to stop classroom copying by libraries in educational establishments.

4.224 **Supposing they are two students at a university requiring the copies for totally different courses?**

This does not seem to matter. They still require them for substantially the same purpose and they are receiving instruction in the same place, although this might not apply if two lecturers asked for the same material for totally different courses.

4.225 **Can the librarian rely on the user's honesty when signing the declaration form?**

Basically, yes, in respect of the purposes for which the copy is required, but certain measures to ensure that the law is complied with must also be in place.

4.226 **Supposing the user signs the declaration and it turns out to be untrue?**

Librarians cannot be expected to know the inner motives of their users and the law recognizes this. The librarian may rely on a signed declaration from the reader as to the purpose for which the copy is required and the truthfulness of the statement that a copy has not been supplied by another librarian previously.

4.227 **Then who is liable if the user signs a false declaration?**

The law specifies that it is the user who would be guilty, as if they had made the copy themselves.

4.228 **How can a librarian know that a copy has not been obtained from another library?**

That is not possible. But the declaration which the user signs specifically states that the user has not been supplied with a copy by you or any other librarian.

4.229   Can the user give the copy to someone else?

Perhaps. But the declaration says that the reader will not use the copy except for non-commercial research or private study. Giving it away could be regarded as using it for other purposes, but this is open to question. What is clear is that if the user gave it to someone else and they used it for any other purpose, this would make it an infringing copy. But the reader signs a declaration to say they will not give a copy of it to anyone else, i.e. they will not give a copy of the copy with which they have been supplied to anyone else. In other words, they will not photocopy the photocopy.

4.230   What happens if the user no longer requires the copy and subsequently gives these copies back to the library?

Unless the library considers itself a prescribed library (see paragraphs 4.256–264) it might be wise to refuse such generosity, although another view is that the copy is perfectly legitimate and can therefore be regarded as having the status of the original and can be given to a non-prescribed library. It would be sensible to document this, just in case its status were questioned.

4.231   Would it be best to destroy such copies?

Not necessarily. The user is entitled to keep the copy and may add it to files of other papers. These are often then deposited in an appropriate department of the institution or company. A suitable registry would need to be used for depositing such material, but see the previous paragraph.

4.232   If a user gives the copy to someone else, can a user have another from the library?

No, because a user must sign to say they have not previously been supplied with a copy.

4.233   Supposing a user genuinely lost the previous copy?

The librarian cannot legally supply another. Readers should not be so careless! However, there seems to be nothing to stop readers borrowing the item and making a further copy for their private use. In this case, the copying would fall outside the provisions for libraries and become fair dealing.

4.234 **What is the position if a second user also genuinely asks for the same material as the first, equally ignorant of the request by the first person?**

If the librarian is aware of this, the second person cannot be supplied with a copy.

4.235 **That seems rather unfair on the second user.**

Perhaps so. But the idea is that a user should share the first person's copy.

4.236 **Do all these references to the 'librarian' really mean only the person in charge of the library?**

No. The law says that references to the librarian include a person acting on behalf of the librarian.

4.237 **Can any librarian make a copy for any member of the public?**

It would appear so, but the declaration form must always be signed to ensure that the conditions for making the copy are met.

4.238 **What about information brokers who obtain documents from libraries for their clients?**

If a broker goes to a library in person to ask for a copy to be made and that copy is for a client, the librarian should not make the copy unless the broker can produce a signed copy of the appropriate declaration form. The broker cannot sign a declaration that the document is required by the broker personally for the purposes of research for a non-commercial purpose or private study.

4.239 **Could the broker be regarded as acting on behalf of the librarian?**

Not really, because the broker will actually be asking the library for the copies.

4.240 **Could the broker collect the properly signed forms on behalf of a client and bring them to the library to request copies?**

This would seem a possible solution but the librarian would need to be sure that the signatures on the forms were actually those of the persons requiring the copies. Signatures of agents are not allowed. However, it is unlikely that a broker would be working for someone wanting copies for a non-commercial purpose, so the scenario would fail on that count if nothing else.

4.241 Can the broker charge for the copies?

No. The broker can recoup the cost through charging for other services but not for the copy itself.

4.242 Must all library users pay?

Yes. All copying done on behalf of someone else by librarians must be paid for.

4.243 What is the point of making people pay?

Basically the idea was introduced to stop publicly funded libraries being overwhelmed by demands for free photocopies. Users enjoyed a privilege but it was not to be funded from the public purse. Unfortunately the law is so framed that the rule applies to all libraries.

4.244 Supposing circumstances are such that the user cannot pay?

Legally, some way must be found for payment to be made. For example, employees in a company or researchers in a university should pay when copies are made for them. They could be reimbursed by the institution later or a voucher system could be introduced, but some kind of payment should be made.

4.245 Is the amount specified?

Not directly, but it must be a sufficient amount not only to cover the cost of making the copy but also to contribute towards the general running costs of the library.

4.246 Is photocopying subject to VAT?

Yes, although the amounts on individual copies may be so small that a per page charge which is calculated to include the VAT is probably the most practicable way to collect this.

4.247 Do users of public libraries have to pay?

Yes. Some people have argued that the payment of local council tax is a contribution to the general expense of the library, but that would only apply to residents of the authority that runs the library and users must still pay for the actual cost of the photocopy.

4.248   What about students?

They should pay, like everyone else, although again, it could be argued that part of their fees is for the general upkeep of the library. Again, they still have to pay for the copies.

4.249   What about people in industrial and commercial companies or government departments? Can they really be expected to pay?

In the case of industrial/commercial companies it is unlikely that library privilege would apply anyway, as copying would almost certainly not be for non-commercial research. In organizations such as government or local authorities, theoretically the user should pay, but in practice this becomes impossible. The money goes to the library, not the copyright owner, anyway, so common sense needs to be used. This book tells you what the law actually says. Implementation is another matter!

Interlibrary supply

4.250   What does the term 'interlibrary' supply mean?

The term 'supply' has been used because it is important to distinguish between lending and copying for interlibrary purposes. For lending between libraries see paragraphs 4.76 and following. Copies supplied between libraries are often referred to as 'interlibrary loans' but they are actually copies supplied for retention. It is also important to distinguish between interlibrary copying, which is intended for one library to supply copies for the collection of another library, and copying for individuals who have made their request to their own library which does not hold the material required and which has therefore transmitted the request to another library. The law makes provision for interlibrary copying but copying by one library for users of another library must be treated as a two-stage process. See the diagram opposite if you are confused!

Interlibrary copying for use by individuals

4.251   What about supplying copies through interlibrary arrangements for individual users?

Either the library which receives the original request must send it on to another library with the declaration form (see paragraphs 4.209 and following) or the library which receives the request must have a clear agreement with the library to which the request is sent that the first library will collect and retain the

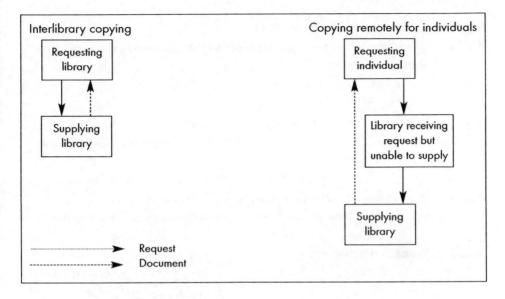

declaration form on behalf of the second library which made the copy. Otherwise the library making the copy has no proof that the copy was made legally.

Example: A researcher in Swatville University asks the librarian for a copy of an article from a periodical which Swatville does not take but which is taken by Sometown University. The librarian of Swatville applies to Sometown University, acting simply as the letterbox for the researcher, who is entitled to ask for copies from Sometown University under the library provisions. The librarian of Swatville University must be aware that Sometown University Library sees the librarian as acting as its agent to handle requests from individuals which are to be passed to Sometown University. So either Swatville sends the request with the user declaration form or there is a proper agreement between Sometown and Swatville that requests sent to Sometown by Swatville will have had the declaration form signed and kept by Swatville University Library.

4.252 How does the British Library Document Supply Centre (BLDSC) manage to supply copies to individuals?

Exactly as described in the previous paragraph. All institutional users of BLDSC services sign just such a declaration to act on behalf of the British Library in this respect. See also Section 10.

Interlibrary copying for library collections

4.253 What about supplying photocopies or microforms of works for library collections?

This is allowed for certain libraries only.

4.254 Which libraries can supply copies, then?

Any library in the United Kingdom can make and supply photocopies of material in its collection.

4.255 What about receiving copies?

Only prescribed libraries may request and receive copies for their collections.

4.256 What is a prescribed library?

A prescribed library for the purposes of receiving copies is carefully defined as any library in the following categories not conducted for profit (see paragraph 4.261):

- any public library which is defined as a library administered by a library authority in England and Wales; a statutory library authority in Scotland or an Education and Library Board in Northern Ireland
- the British Library, the National Libraries of Scotland and Wales, the Bodleian Library (Oxford) and the University Library, Cambridge
- libraries in educational establishments
- parliamentary and government libraries
- local authority libraries
- any library whose purpose is to facilitate or encourage study of a wide range of given topics (see paragraph 4.260)
- any library whose purpose is to facilitate or encourage study of a wide range of given topics and which is outside the United Kingdom.

4.257 What constitutes an educational establishment?

Educational establishment is defined broadly as any school, college, polytechnic or university in the public sector, but for specific details see Statutory Instrument 2005/223 and paragraph 4.178.

4.258 Is a government library restricted to those in Civil Service departments?

No, the definition includes any library conducted for or administered by an agency which is administered by a Minister of the Crown. So, for example, the library of an NHS hospital would count as a government library. The library of a private hospital would not.

4.259 **What is the difference between a public library and a library administered by a local authority?**

This latter category covers those libraries which act as libraries for departments of local or county councils. For example, many planning or environmental health departments have their own libraries and some councils have a members' library for councillors' benefit.

4.260 **What is this 'wide range of given topics' just mentioned?**

It is actually listed as 'bibliography, education, fine arts, history, languages, law, literature, medicine, music, philosophy, religion, sciences (including natural and social science) or technology'.

4.261 **What exactly does 'conducted for profit' mean?**

This is a very important phrase, as it does not apply simply to the library itself but includes the organization which owns or administers the library. So the library of a major industrial company may well not be conducted for profit but the owning company certainly is, and the library is therefore not a prescribed library.

4.262 **What about charities?**

The library of a charity may or may not be a prescribed library, depending on the purpose of the charity. If it is a charity whose aims are primarily to facilitate or encourage the study of the range of topics stated, then the library can claim to be prescribed. If the charity is mainly concerned with other purposes, such as improving social welfare, advancing human rights or promoting particular points of view, or if the charity operates commercially, then it cannot claim to be prescribed.

4.263 **What about libraries of learned societies?**

Many of these will qualify, as the primary aim of the society will be to facilitate or encourage the study of the relevant subject. But, like charities, it will depend on the aims of the society administering the library.

4.264 **What about private libraries?**

Some private libraries could say that they are conducted for profit, and in those cases they cannot qualify, but others are charitable in status and, again, it will depend on the nature of the charity.

4.265 Are the rules for libraries that can supply copies different?

Yes. Any library (whether conducted for profit or not) can supply a copy through interlibrary arrangements but cannot receive a copy.

4.266 Can anything be copied by prescribed libraries?

No. There are restrictions on both periodical articles and books (monographs).

4.267 What are the restrictions?

First, no library may be supplied with more than one copy of any material. Second, no library may be supplied with a copy of more than one article from a periodical issue or even part of a non-periodical work unless the requesting library also supplies a written statement to the effect that it is a prescribed library and does not know, and has not been able by reasonable enquiry to find out, the name and address of someone entitled to authorize the making of the copy. Third, the requesting library must pay.

4.268 What does 'reasonable enquiry' mean?

This is not defined, but it should be remembered that, as the library which is being asked to make the copy must hold the material, it is quite possible that the requesting library could obtain the required information from the supplying library, and even more likely that the supplying library could find this out anyway. However, if the material is published by a company now out of business or in a remote corner of the world and the publisher does not reply to correspondence, then the copies can be made, but there is always a remote chance that the copyright owner may appear and challenge what has been done. Nothing is certain in the world of copyright!

4.269 Who is the person entitled to authorize the making of the copy?

As the requirement is to make a copy of all or a substantial part of the work, the publisher will probably be the only person who can authorize the making of such a copy, as publishers usually own the copyright in the total publication (as against authors, who own the content of the text, illustrators, who own rights in their work, etc.). However, modern publishing contracts are usually for fixed, often short terms, so many rights in individual parts of the monograph may have reverted to the author. However, the publisher will still own the typographical copyright.

4.270   Is a prescribed library allowed to keep the copies and add them to stock?

Yes. This is one way that the problem of two people requiring the same material can be overcome. Reader A borrows the photocopy and returns it. Reader B then borrows it in the same way as any other library materials.

4.271   What if a copy is lost or destroyed?

On the face of it, a second copy could not possibly be asked for as prescribed libraries may only request one copy and there is no time limit on this. However, it is a nice point that, if the photocopy has been placed in the permanent collection, then the library may be able to request a replacement at some distant date, as the first photocopy is legitimate and can be regarded as part of the permanent collection. See paragraph 4.283.

4.272   Can the library subsequently dispose of the copy to another library?

It seems probable that this can be done only to another prescribed library which did not already have a copy of the material in question, but whether this second library would also have to pay the stipulated amount is open to question.

4.273   Suppose the library sold off its collection. What should happen to the photocopies?

They should either be sold to another prescribed library (which should pay the cost of making the copies, plus a contribution to the running expenses of the library) or destroyed.

4.274   Must libraries pay for interlibrary copying?

Yes, but the conditions are slightly different. In this case the requesting library must pay a sum equivalent to but not exceeding the cost of making the copy, plus a contribution to the general running expenses of the library.

4.275   Can the fees be waived?

There is no provision in the law to waive the fees.

4.276   Does interlibrary copying attract VAT?

Yes, just as copying for individuals does.

4.277   How can a library which is not a prescribed library obtain a photocopy on interlibrary loan?

Libraries that are not prescribed libraries may not request material from other libraries for their collections but only for individuals for non-commercial purposes.

4.278   Can the non-prescribed library keep the copy?

This is most improbable, as the copy had to be made for a non-commercial purpose and most non-prescribed libraries are functioning in a commercial context, although the law is not clear. Copies can only be requested for the use of individuals and must be handed over to them, but if they have then acquired the same status as the original it may be possible to do with them anything that could be done with the original, which would include donating it to any kind of library. If this happens, the actions should be clearly documented to show that the non-prescribed library behaved properly.

4.279   What about brokers who request items through interlibrary copying for their clients?

The broker cannot easily do this. However, the broker could simply be acting as a letterbox for the client as an individual or could enter into a proper agreement with a library to be its agent. The client would have to give assurances that the material was always for non-commercial research and would have to sign a declaration on each occasion to that effect.

4.280   Can the broker charge for the copies obtained through interlibrary loan?

No. This would be dealing in the copies, which is an infringement. The broker can, however, charge for other services and so recoup the costs necessarily incurred in obtaining the document through interlibrary loan.

Copying for preservation

Note that for preservation purposes archives are included in the law as well as libraries.

4.281   Can any library or archive copy for preservation purposes?

No. It must be prescribed (see paragraph 4.256).

4.282 **Can prescribed libraries or archives copy their own materials under these conditions?**

Yes, so long as the stipulated conditions are fulfilled. See 4.283 and following.

4.283 **Can anything in a prescribed library or archive be copied?**

No. First, material has to be in the permanent collection of the library or archive. Therefore it is not allowed to borrow a document from somewhere else, put it into the collection on a temporary basis, copy it and then return it to the original owner. This is particularly important for collections which are deposited for limited periods (e.g. lifetime of the owner). Second, the material has to be in the permanent collection and available only for reference on the premises or for loan only to other libraries or archives. Third, it must not be reasonably practicable for the library or archive to purchase a copy.

4.284 **Is it permitted to make more than one copy for preservation?**

This seems unlikely. The Act says 'a copy' may be made.

4.285 **Must the copy be on paper or can the preservation copy be in digital form?**

As the Act defines copying as including making electronic copies (see paragraphs 4.30–35) there seems no reason why a preservation copy cannot be digital.

Copying for replacement of lost items

4.286 **Sometimes materials in the permanent reference collection are lost, damaged or destroyed. Can copies of this material be obtained from other libraries?**

Theft, careless use or fire are all examples of how this might happen. In these circumstances replacement copies can be obtained from other libraries or archives.

4.287 **Which libraries and archives are concerned?**

First, for supplying copies for preservation and replacement, any library or archive in the United Kingdom. Second, for requesting and receiving copies, any prescribed library or any archive not conducted for profit and not forming part of, or administered by, an organization conducted for profit. Note that here the limitations for archives are different from those for libraries, which set out specific classes of library. So the archive of a charity whose primary aim was, say, social welfare would be a prescribed archive but the library of the same charity would not. So, the archive of a major chemical company could copy material to replace that in a university library, but the reverse is not true.

4.288 For exactly what reasons can material be copied for replacement?

The law allows copying in order to replace an item in the permanent collection for reference purposes only, to replace material in another library or archive which has been lost, damaged or destroyed. Clearly a library or archive cannot replace material in its own collection in this way, since, if it is lost or destroyed, it is not there to copy!

4.289 Can one library or archive copy for another?

Yes, as long as the requesting library or archive provides a declaration to the effect that it is a prescribed library or archive, that it has not been practicable to purchase a copy, that the copy is required as a replacement for an item in the permanent collection which has been lost, damaged or destroyed and that the copy will be used for reference purposes only. In addition, the requesting library or archive must pay as set out in paragraphs 4.274 and following.

4.290 Once the material has been copied, can it be used like other materials in a library or archive?

Yes, provided that it is added to the permanent collection.

4.291 So what about books or periodicals in general lending collections which are falling apart or are lost?

These cannot qualify for copying under these special regulations. Replacement copies must be bought from the publisher, where available, or a copy obtained from another library if the conditions for doing so are met (i.e. the publisher cannot be traced and a copy cannot easily be purchased).

4.292 Could a prescribed library or archive obtain a copy of a work from a library if the work was in the general lending collection of the supplying library or archive?

Yes, provided that the copy being made was for use only in the permanent reference collection or in a collection available for lending to other libraries (but not to individuals).

Copying unpublished works

4.293 **Can unpublished materials in a library or archive be copied for users?**

Yes, under certain conditions.

4.294 **What are the conditions?**

First, that the work was not published before the document was deposited. Second, copying may not take place if the author has prohibited this.

Example: Edward Gotrip writes a novel in the hope he will become famous and deposits the manuscript with the local public library. Subsequently it is published. The public library is entitled to copy the manuscript even though the text has become a published novel. However, Una Suming has her book published and then, having become famous, deposits the manuscript with the local public library, but no copying of it is allowed.

4.295 **Can the librarian or archivist plead ignorance of the fact that the author had prohibited copying?**

Not really. The law says that copies may not be made when the author has prohibited this, and the librarian or archivist knows, or ought to know, that this is the case. Therefore it is sensible to keep a register of deposited unpublished material, with notes on any items which the author has prohibited the library or archive from copying.

4.296 **Can whole works be copied, or only parts?**

The law allows copying of the whole of an unpublished document.

4.297 **Can unpublished works be copied for anyone?**

Yes, provided that the reader signs a declaration to say that the documents are required only for non-commercial research or private study and a copy has not previously been supplied to the reader, that the documents were not published before they were deposited and that the reader pays a sum which covers the cost of making the copy and a contribution to the general running costs of the library or archive.

4.298 **Can they have more than one copy?**

No person may have more than one copy of any work.

4.299   Do users have to pay?

Yes, they must pay, just as in paragraphs 4.242–7.

4.300   Do the restrictions on not supplying copies to more than one person for substantially the same purpose at substantially the same time apply?

No, these restrictions are not laid down for unpublished works.

4.301   Is there a standard declaration form as for published materials?

Yes. The text is published in Statutory Instrument 89/1212 Schedule 2 Form B (as amended in 2003) and also in Appendix 3 of this book.

4.302   Can copies be supplied from one library or archive to another?

No. Copying between libraries and archives applies only to published works and the sections of the Act on unpublished works allow copying only for individuals. It would seem likely, by analogy with a user of a non-prescribed library, that the user of a library or archive could ask that library or archive to apply on their behalf for a copy of an unpublished work, but they would have to sign the appropriate declaration form, pay the required amount and also retain the copy for personal use, not present it to the library or archive which has acted as intermediary for them.

Abstracts

4.303   Does the abstract that goes with a journal article have a separate copyright?

Yes. It is a distinct work which can stand alone, otherwise it is not really an abstract.

4.304   Can any abstract be copied?

Yes, but not those which are prepared specifically for abstracting services, such as *Chemical Abstracts*. The law says that abstracts which accompany articles on scientific or technical subjects may be copied, provided that there is no licensing scheme, but just what 'scientific or technical' means is open for discussion.

4.305   Can the abstract be copied with the article?

Yes. The law states that such abstracts can be copied freely unless there is a licensing scheme which covers them, in which case you must belong to the scheme in order to copy the abstracts. So far no such scheme has been devised.

4.306 How about writing abstracts for information services?

It is quite in order to prepare abstracts from scratch by summarizing the article concerned, using your skill and knowledge to read the article and present the information in a different form. You should not use actual text from the original article. Once the abstract has been written, the copyright belongs to you or your employer, as appropriate.

4.307 Can abstracts be used in information services?

Yes. They can be copied, distributed electronically, printed, given away or sold, either freely or by licence.

Copying as a condition of export

4.308 Supposing a library or archive contains material which is still in copyright but is of considerable national interest and it is decided to sell this abroad, can anything be done to copy it before it is taken out of the country?

Sometimes, yes. If the condition of export is that a copy is made to be retained in this country it is not an infringement to make the copy or to receive it to be kept in a library or archive.

Public administration

4.309 Are there any other reasons for being allowed to copy?

Yes. Another reason is what the Act calls public administration.

4.310 What does 'public administration' cover?

Not as much as it would at first seem! The Act gives four areas, namely:

- parliamentary proceedings
- judicial proceedings
- Royal Commission
- statutory inquiry.

4.311   **What can be copied?**

There are no limits. The Act says: 'Copyright is not infringed by anything done for the purposes of Parliamentary or judicial proceedings.' The only qualification is a further allowance to the effect that if anything is copied for the proceedings and subsequently published in those proceedings. that is not in itself an infringement of copyright.

4.312   **What about Freedom of Information?**

Freedom of Information is not mentioned in the CDPA, as it was not a government policy then. There is a real problem, because the CDPA says that it is not an infringement to copy something if an Act of Parliament requires it. But the Freedom of Information Act does not require material to be copied – it requires only that the information be provided.

4.313   **So can material be copied to answer a Freedom of Information request?**

The strict interpretation of the Act says 'no' but the Lord Chancellor issued a guidance note to say that where it was necessary to copy a document in order to answer an FOI request, that document could be copied without infringing copyright, provided that it was clearly stated on the copy supplied that it was for an FOI request and that any further use of that copy would constitute infringement of copyright.

Material open to public inspection

4.314   **Many libraries contain registers of various kinds and often act as a public information point for local authority activity such as planning applications or electoral registers. Can any of this material be copied?**

When material is open to the public as part of a statutory requirement, or is on a statutory register, any material in it which contains factual information can be copied without infringing the copyright in it as a literary work, so long as this is done with the authority of the appropriate person and copies are not issued to the public.

4.315   **What constitutes factual information?**

Exactly that. Anything in the material which is opinion or argument for or against a case would not be covered by this allowance.

4.316   Does making a copy for a member of the public constitute 'issuing copies to the public'?

No. Making single copies for individuals in this way is outside the definition of 'issuing copies to the public'.

4.317   Can a member of the public copy an electoral register?

Yes, and the limits are not set down legally, although there may be physical or financial restraints to consider if large quantities are needed. Where whole registers are wanted it would be better for a reader to contact the local Registrar.

4.318   Are all forms of the electoral register available to be copied?

No. The full register is available only to a limited number of organizations, such as local councils, the police and similar agencies. It is not publicly available and cannot be copied. The publicly available version contains only those names of members of the public who have not asked for their names to be withheld from the public register, and this shorter version can be copied.

4.319   Supposing someone wants to inspect some documents in this class but lives some way away and cannot come to consult the documents?

Any amount of the material may be copied for such persons, provided that the appropriate person gives authorization.

4.320   Who is an 'appropriate person'?

An appropriate person is the person who is required to make the material open to the public or the person maintaining the register. Such persons can authorize libraries and others to make copies as described above.

4.321   Does this apply to maps and plans as well?

Yes. There is no restriction on the material which may be copied for those needing to have it sent to them to exercise their rights. However, to prevent misuse, any maps supplied for this purpose must be marked with a statement to the effect that the maps have been supplied under the Copyright Act for the purposes of consulting publicly available material and must not be further copied without permission. The full text of this statement, which must be used as it stands, is printed in SI 89/1099. (Interestingly, the Statutory Instrument refers to statutory registers, but the relevant sections of the Act do not.)

4.322   Does this also apply to statutory registers, such as registers of voters?

Apparently not, because no mention is made of statutory registers in the relevant section of the Act. However, the Statutory Instrument does refer specifically to statutory registers in this section, so it is unclear just what is allowed.

4.323   Do these regulations apply only to United Kingdom materials?

Mostly, yes. The two exceptions are material made open to the public by the European Patent Office and the World Intellectual Property Organization, both intended to assist the process of patent registration.

4.324   What about material which constitutes public records?

Any material which constitutes public records under the appropriate Public Records Acts and which is open to public inspection can be copied and the copies supplied to anyone, with the authority of the appropriate officer as appointed under the relevant Acts of Parliament.

4.325   What if an Act of Parliament actually requires that something be copied for the processes of law?

If the copying is a required part of an Act of Parliament, then it is not an infringement of copyright.

4.326   Supposing a copy is needed because of a national crisis, such as war?

This may be allowed as being in the public interest. The Act says that nothing shall be done or prevented which the rule of law requires for the national interest.

4.327   Does the existence of a separate typographical copyright prevent libraries and others from copying materials?

No. The law specifically states that anything that can be done with a copyright work by way of copying can also be done to the typographical layout of that work.

Visually impaired persons

4.328 **Supposing someone needs to use a work that is in printed form but they have a visual disability that prevents them from reading it. Can copies be made for them?**

Fortunately, legislation permits copies to be made for visually impaired people.

4.329 **Who qualifies as a visually impaired person?**

The definition is broader than might be expected. It is: 'A visually impaired person is one who is blind or partially sighted or has uncorrectable sight-loss or who has a physical disability which makes it impossible for them to hold a book or move their eyes.'

4.330 **How much may be copied?**

The whole of a work may be copied into a format suitable for the visually impaired person (VIP) to use.

4.331 **What formats can be used?**

The law does not specify or limit the formats to be used.

4.332 **Are there any restrictions?**

Yes, a number of limitations are put on this exception. They are as follows:

- the VIP must have lawful possession of a copy of the work or lawful access to it
- the work must not be commercially available in the format needed
- if the work is a musical work, transfer to an alternative format does not involve recording a performance of the work
- the copy made must have sufficient acknowledgement of its source (bibliographic reference would seem to be implied)
- the copy must be marked to show that it was made under the legislation relating to making copies for VIPs.

4.333 **What does 'lawful access' mean?**

While it is not defined, it would seem that, if the work is in a reference library to which the VIP has regular access, this would be acceptable.

4.334 Can a library or other organization charge for making the copy?

Yes, but not more than the actual cost of making it.

4.335 Can one VIP pass the copy on to another?

Yes, provided that the second person fulfils all the criteria set out in paragraph 4.332. But they must not copy the copy they have and pass that on instead.

4.336 What if several students in a school, college or university all need copies in alternative formats?

The copies can be made provided the institution making the copies has lawful possession of an original copy of the work. The other conditions set out for copying for individuals in paragraph 4.332 also apply. In addition, if the institution making the copy is an educational establishment (see paragraph 4.178), then it must make sure that the copies are used only for educational purposes.

4.337 Making these copies can be costly. Can the institution keep an electronic file so as to make copies for other students in the future?

Yes, this is allowed, with some restrictions.

4.338 What are these restrictions?

In addition to the conditions set out for individuals in paragraph 4.332 the institution making the copy must:

- keep records of the copies made and to whom they are supplied
- keep records of any intermediate copies lent to other institutions
- allow the copyright owner or their representative (perhaps the CLA) access to these records
- notify the copyright owner or representative of any copies transferred or lent to other organizations.

4.339 Does this mean that the copies in alternative formats can be lent?

Yes, but only to another organization fulfilling all the criteria set out earlier.

4.340   **Are there any other rules?**

One important rule is that when the original is in electronic form and contains electronic management data about ownership, authorship or other information, any copies made in electronic form must also contain this information and it must not be deleted.

4.341   **What about licences?**

Where a licensing scheme offers the facility to make copies in alternative formats this licence must be adhered to. Also the publishing industry has issued helpful guidelines on copying for visually impaired people which are less restrictive and cumbersome than the law. See www.pls.org.uk for more details.

4.342   **What is the advantage of copying under licence rather than just making the copies?**

Where multiple copies are needed, the use of the licence saves a lot of bureaucratic paperwork and record keeping.

Section 5
Artistic works

Definition

5.1   What is the definition of an artistic work?

The definition of artistic works includes:

- graphic works such as paintings, drawings, diagrams, maps, charts and plans, engravings, lithographs, etchings or woodcuts
- sculpture
- collage
- photographs (including slides and negatives as well as microforms)
- architectural works (including buildings of any kind)
- works of artistic craftsmanship such as jewellery or pottery.

5.2   Does a slide count as a photograph?

Yes. Slides are protected in the same way as photographs because a photograph is defined thus: 'photograph' means a recording of light or other radiation on any medium on which an image is produced or from which an image may by any means be produced, and which is not part of a film.

5.3   Are overhead transparencies (OHPs) protected by copyright?

This depends on whether they contain original material prepared by the lecturer or whether they are simply copies of something that already existed such as a table from a book. In the former case they may be copyright if the work is original enough. If they are a copy of something else, then they may be photographs, in which case they will be copyright in their own right. But if they are photographs of something still in copyright, then they can be made only with the copyright owner's permission.

5.4   Do microforms qualify for copyright?

Certainly. A microfilm or microfiche ('microform' for short) is a photograph and attracts copyright in the same way as a photograph. A microfilm containing several different documents may also be a database (see Section 9).

5.5 What happens if the work which has been microfilmed is still in copyright?

There are then two copyrights, one in the original document and one in the microform. To make a new copy of the microform would require the consent of the original copyright owner.

5.6 Supposing the work that has been microfilmed is out of copyright?

There is probably still copyright in the microform as a photograph, even though the photographed work is out of copyright. Some authorities argue that there is no copyright in the photograph of a 'flat' object such as a document, but others would argue that change of medium (from paper to photograph) requires sufficient skill to create a new original work.

Example: A microform of Magna Carta would attract copyright as a photograph, but the Magna Carta itself certainly would not.

5.7 What is the situation if enlargements are made from the microform?

The enlargements can be an infringement of copyright in the microform and the original document, if the original is still in copyright, or of just the microform if that is still in copyright but the document filmed is not.

5.8 Supposing a library wishes to make microform copies of works in its collection to preserve them?

This is in order only if the original documents are out of copyright or if they come under the special provisions for preservation (see paragraphs 4.281 and following).

Authors and their rights

5.9 Who counts as the author of an artistic work?

The author of an artistic work is defined in the same terms as for a literary, dramatic or musical work (see paragraphs 4.13 and following). This includes, in the case of photographs, the photographer.

5.10 **Do authors of artistic works have moral rights?**

Yes. They are described in paragraphs 3.2–3.7. Note that authors of artistic works have the right to be named as the authors if the works are exhibited in public. This right has to be asserted before the exhibition takes place in order to be valid.

Ownership of copyright

5.11 **Who owns the copyright in an artistic work?**

Generally, ownership of the copyright of an artistic work is defined in the same terms as for a literary, dramatic or musical work (see paragraphs 3.8; 4.27 and following). But note that the ownership of commissioned paintings, photographs or engravings made before 1 August 1989 belongs to the person commissioning the work if they actually paid for it to be done, not just expenses. See also paragraphs 3.19 and 4.27 for unpublished works bequeathed to libraries, archives, galleries or museums.

5.12 **Who owns the copyright in a collection of slides?**

Each slide has its own copyright, just like the articles in a periodical (see paragraph 3.24). However, there will also be a copyright in a compilation made up of slides. It may also be a database (see Section 9), depending on the way the collection is put together.

5.13 **If a library or archive makes its own microforms or digital copies, who owns the copyright?**

The copyright belongs to the library or archive. However, if the library/archive commissions an outside bureau to make the copies, ownership of the copyright will depend on the contract between the two parties. Where the copies have been bought from a commercial company, the copyright will remain with that company, despite the status of the original documents filmed.

5.14 **Quite often copies of photographs supplied by libraries or archives state that, although they are old, the copyright is owned by the library or archive, from whom permission must be sought to make copies or publish the photograph. Is this legal?**

The position is that the library or archive owns the photographs but not necessarily the copyright in them. It may well impose restrictions on the subsequent use of the photographs and that is its right as owner of the physical photographs. But it may not own the copyright in these works. If conditions are imposed, such as payment for publication, then, once these are met, the library or archive has no further claim on the photograph and certainly not the copyright in it.

Owners' rights

5.15 What rights does the owner of copyright in artistic works have?

The owner has the same rights as for literary, dramatic or musical works (see Section 4). Note that exhibiting an artistic work is not a right that the copyright owner enjoys, despite general belief to the contrary. This is not true for literary, dramatic or musical works (see paragraph 4.43).

5.16 Do people who appear in photographs have any rights over them?

Not under copyright law, but this is an area where particular care needs to be exercised. Although the person taking the photograph owns the copyright (or their employer if appropriate) the use of that photograph may be restricted by other legal considerations. For example, using the image of a famous person to promote a product or event can lead to claims of loss of revenue, because the celebrity would have made a charge for having their name used in this way even if the copyright in the photograph is owned by the person using it. Even more important can be the use of photographs which depict people in private situations such as in their home, in hospital or even receiving medical attention in the street. The situation is public but the event is private, and people have sued for use of photographs under human rights legislation in these circumstances. Use of general street scenes or groups is probably acceptable.

Copying artistic works

5.17 What about taking photographs?

A photograph of an artistic work (say a statue or painting) is an infringement of the artist's copyright unless the work is a building, a sculpture or a work of artistic craftsmanship and is on permanent public display in a public open space or premises open to the public.

5.18 What counts as a work of artistic craftsmanship?

The law does not give a definition but the courts have generally (although exceptions can be found) ruled that the work must demonstrate craftsmanship in the making of it and some artistic merit in terms of being appealing to the eye. All rather subjective, and different judgements give different slants on these ideas!

5.19   What constitutes 'open to the public'?

This is not defined but it would certainly be a street or thoroughfare and any building to which the public had access in the normal course of events. Presumably a library, museum or art gallery is open to the public, although particular parts of it may not be, so these would not count (e.g. strongrooms, vaults, closed stacks, etc.). Rooms in town halls and other similar buildings are more difficult to define.

5.20   What constitutes 'permanent'?

Unfortunately this is not defined. Obviously something on loan for, say, six months, could not be permanent. Something might be on display for six months and then taken away but be counted as permanent because it was intended to be so when it was put on display in the first place.

5.21   The owners of some buildings charge copying fees to photograph artistic works housed in them even though the works must surely be out of copyright. Is this allowed?

This is not a copyright fee but a copying fee. The owners of a cathedral, for example, cannot claim there is copyright in a medieval painting but this does not stop them from charging for the privilege of access to photograph their property. The painting is their property even though the copyright has long since expired.

5.22   What about making a photographic image of a painting?

Photocopying, microfilming or making a transparency, slide or digital image of a drawing, engraving or painting are all infringements.

5.23   What about making a model of something in a painting?

It is also an infringement to make a three-dimensional model of a picture, photograph or painting, in just the same way that photographing a statue is an infringement.

5.24   Would the model be protected by copyright?

That is hard to say. If it is an exact model, then it could be argued that it is not copyright because, although skill and labour had been used to make it, there was no actual original creativity. However, if the model was selective in the detail

89

reproduced (say a small model of a ship) or if it had been scaled up or down, then it might be possible to argue that not only craftsmanship but also technical skill had been used and so the model qualified for copyright. Even if the original was out of copyright, the model could still qualify.

5.25   What happens if a photograph (or television programme) happens to include a piece of copyright material in the background? Say an interview in front of a recent painting in a gallery?

Incidental copying of this nature is not an infringement, but it would be if the photographer or TV producer deliberately intended the painting or sculpture to be included. However, if the programme were about a particular painter whose works were still in copyright, then the inclusion would be deliberate and would infringe the artist's copyright. There might still be a defence of using the image for criticism or review, but it would depend on the nature of the programme.

5.26   Supposing the library/archive holds a painting which it wishes to reproduce as a slide, poster or postcard?

If the painting is out of copyright or if the picture is of a statue or something similar on permanent public display, then there is no problem. Remember that the slide, poster or postcard will attract copyright, which will be owned by the photographer or the library/archive, depending on whether the photographer was an employee of the library/archive or the library/archive simply commissioned the taking of the photograph!

5.27   Supposing there is an exhibition of children's work and the library wants to use this for publicity material or to publish it?

Technically, the copyright belongs to the children individually and the permission of each child or guardian is necessary before works can be reproduced. Some teachers might argue that the copyright belongs to the school, but the child is not employed there (at least not in the sense of gainful employment!), and the teacher cannot claim the copyright, because the child actually did the painting.

Issuing copies to the public
5.28   Does issuing to the public apply to artistic works?

Issuing copies to the public is restricted as for literary, dramatic and musical works (see paragraphs 4.39 and following).

Performing the work

5.29 Is it an infringement to perform an artistic work?

There is no performing right, including the right of exhibition, for artistic works.

5.30 Can the owner of a painting or other artistic work put it on public display?

Yes. The right of display is not one of the acts restricted by copyright. Once the work has been purchased the owner of the work may display it, but this does not alter the rights of the copyright owner to reproduce the work, e.g. on postcards, photographs, slides, etc. But note that exhibiting an anonymous copyright artistic work which has not been previously published or exhibited has the effect of starting the period of copyright protection all over again, to 70 years from first exhibiting the work.

Communicating the work to the public by electronic means

5.31 Supposing a television programme included a shot of a painting or sculpture. Would this be counted as broadcasting?

Yes, unless it was incidentally included, as mentioned in paragraph 5.25.

5.32 Supposing the television programme is a news item about an artist whose recent death is being reported?

Then, to include one of the artist's paintings as part of the news might not be an infringement, because this would be reporting current events (see paragraph 5.62).

5.33 If I want to put a photograph or picture on a website, must I obtain permission from the copyright owner?

Yes, unless it is out of copyright. Putting anything on a website is 'communicating the work to the public by electronic means' and is an infringement of the copyright owner's rights.

Adaptation and translation

5.34 Is there a right of adaptation in artistic works? How does it work?

Yes. Most forms of adaptation are really copying. For example, to make a model of a painting is really an adaptation of the original to a different form, as mentioned under 'models' (paragraphs 5.23–24). For example, making a three-dimensional 'touchy-feely' version of a map would infringe, as it is making a three-dimensional work from a two-dimensional one.

Lending and rental

5.35   Are artistic works subject to lending and rental restrictions?
Yes.

5.36   Does this mean that libraries, archives and galleries may no longer lend artistic works?
Not altogether. In the first place, this restriction applies only to material acquired on or after 1 December 1996. Second, lending (i.e. charging no more than operational costs) is allowed for any library except a public library.

5.37   Why are public libraries excluded?
Because the Act specifically states that public libraries, whether or not a charge is made, cannot lend these materials, except those acquired before December 1996 or under licence.

5.38   Supposing there is no licensing scheme available?
The Secretary of State has the power to implement a scheme subject to appropriate payment as determined by the Copyright Tribunal if necessary.

Publication right

5.39   Does publication right apply to artistic works?
Yes, see paragraphs 4.91 and following.

Typographical copyright

5.40   Does typographical copyright apply to artistic works?
It will depend on the nature of the work. It would be hard to argue that there was typographical arrangement in a photograph or plate of an artistic work, but there would be typographical arrangement in a map, for example. So it would apply in that case.

Duration of copyright

5.41   How long does copyright in artistic works last?

Although artistic works are protected in the same way as literary, dramatic or musical works there are some important differences. Some of the rules are repeated here for ease of reference. The rules about extended and revived copyright described in paragraphs 3.8 and 3.25–3.26 also apply to artistic works.

5.42   Do the rules about works originating in the EEA (see paragraph 4.101 and following) also apply?

Yes, the rules in this area are the same. To save unnecessary repetition the term '70 years' has been used in the following paragraphs but marked * to remind you that the EEA/non-EEA rules apply.

5.43   Are there differences for published and unpublished works?

Yes. Most published artistic works are protected for 70* years from the end of the year in which the author died, so it is important to examine each type of work separately.

Anonymous/pseudonymous artistic works – published

5.44   How long does copyright in anonymous/pseudonymous works last?

Essentially, copyright in these works lasts for 70* years from the end of the year in which they were created, but if they were published during that period, then for 70* years from the end of the year in which they were first made available to the public.

Anonymous/pseudonymous works – unpublished

5.45   Works created after 1 January 1969 are protected for 70* years from the end of the year in which they were created or in which they were first made available to the public. However, where a work was created before 1 August 1989 copyright protection must last until December 31 2039, regardless of the assumed date of creation.

5.46   Is 'first made available to the public' the same as 'published'?

No. In the case of artistic works it includes:

- exhibition
- included in a broadcast or cable television programme
- included in a film.

5.47 Engravings – published

If published after artist's death and before 1 January 1969: protected until year of publication + 50 years. Otherwise protected until year of artist's death + 70* years.

5.48 Engravings – unpublished

Unpublished and the artist died before 1 January 1969: protected until 31 December 2039. Otherwise protected from year of artist's death + 70* years.

5.49 Typographical arrangement

If typographical copyright subsists in the work, it will expire 25 years from the end of the year of first publication.

5.50 Photographs

Photographs formerly had a very complex set of rules governing expiry of copyright but the term of protection has now been standardized at year of photographer's death plus 70 years, or, if anonymous, 70* years from creation, or, if made available to the public, 70* years from the end of the year in which that first took place.

5.51 Unpublished works with an author – generally

Works of which the creator died before 1 January 1969 and which were unpublished are protected until 31 December 2039. All other works are protected for 70* years from the end of the year in which the author died.

Microforms

5.52 How long is a microform or digital image protected?

If the author can be established, for 70* years from the year of the author's death; otherwise 70* years from the year in which the image was made available to the public.

Crown and Parliamentary copyright

5.53 **What about the duration of Crown and Parliamentary copyright?**

Where copyright in an artistic work (other than an engraving or photograph) is owned by the Crown and the work was made before 1 August 1989, copyright expires 50 years from the end of the year in which the work was created. This is very useful for maps, as Ordnance Survey paper maps created more than 50 years ago are out of copyright. Works made after this date are subject to the same rules as literary works (see paragraphs 4.118 and following). Copyright in published engravings made before 1 August 1989 expires 50 years from the year of publication. Copyright in an unpublished engraving made before 1 August 1989 expires on 31 December 2039. However, in the case of unpublished photographs, copyright in those taken on or after 1 August 1989 will last for 125 years, subject to their not being published commercially within the first 75 years; those taken on or after 1 June 1957 but before 1 August 1989 would have protection until the end of 2039; and those taken before 1 June 1957 had protection for 50 years from the end of the year in which they were taken and are therefore now out of copyright.

Works in which the copyright is owned by either or both Houses of Parliament expires at the end of 50 years from the year in which the work was created.

Exceptions

5.54 **Are artistic works subject to the same exceptions as literary works?**

Yes, but there are some differences.

Fair dealing

5.55 **Are artistic works subject to fair dealing?**

Artistic works are subject to fair dealing in a similar way to literary, dramatic and musical works, but there are some differences.

5.56 **What constitutes fair dealing in an artistic work?**

This is undefined as for other works. However, the same general rules apply (see paragraphs 4.130 and following).

5.57 **Do the reasons for fair dealing – non-commercial research or private study; criticism or review; and reporting current events – still apply to artistic works?**

Yes. The reasons are just the same. And the restriction on research being for a non-commercial purpose applies to artistic works as well. The one area where the rules are different is reporting current events.

Research for a non-commercial purpose

5.58 **How can something be copied fairly when it is an artistic work? Surely the whole of the work would be copied?**

Perhaps. Fair dealing does not exclude copying all of the work.

Example: An art student needs to study the different ways of portraying Hercules. The student could take photographs of modern statues, paintings and drawings for personal use to carry out the research. The photographs must not be sold or published, otherwise this would not constitute fair dealing for the purposes of research. If they were subsequently sold or published this would be an infringement, as they would not be fair dealing copies and might be in direct competition with the commercial exploitation of the work by the owner, such as producing postcards. If copies of Hercules that met the student's needs were available commercially, then this copying could be considered unfair.

5.59 **What about people who go to art galleries (and libraries) and make paintings of other people's paintings?**

This would be considered as fair, because it is for private study. The copy would have had sufficient original input from the copying painter to qualify for copyright protection in its own right, but might still be challenged as an infringement of the copyright in the original work.

5.60 **Can a student include a copy of an artistic work, say a photograph of a statue, in a thesis?**

Yes. This is for research, and also providing the answer to an examination, so it is covered by educational copying (see paragraph 4.173). But if the thesis is published, then the copyright in the artistic work is infringed.

Private study

5.61 **Are the rules for private study and artistic works the same as for literary works?**

Yes, the rules are the same. See paragraphs 4.143 and following.

Reporting current events

5.62 **Can artistic works be used to report current events?**

For general conditions see paragraphs 4.158 and following, but note that photographs may not be used for this purpose.

Criticism or review

5.63 **Can artistic works be used in criticism or review?**

Artistic works may be reproduced for criticism or review provided that there is sufficient acknowledgement of their authorship.

5.64 **What constitutes sufficient acknowledgement?**

This is not defined but would presumably include the name of the author, at least.

5.65 **Can an artistic work be reproduced in a journal article?**

Only if the purpose is criticism or review. Simply to include a photograph of a copyright painting to illustrate a point about modern art would not be sufficient justification.

5.66 **What about using a painting or photograph of a piece of sculpture to advertise an exhibition?**

This would not be allowed.

5.67 **What about sale catalogues which include photographs of copyright materials?**

This is allowed. There is a specific clause allowing the copying of works to advertise them for sale.

Educational copying

See also paragraphs 4.164 and following on literary, dramatic and musical works and paragraph 8.23 for use in VLEs.

5.68 May artistic works be copied for educational purposes?

Artistic works may be copied by either the teacher or the student themselves so long as a reprographic process is not used.

Example: A teacher or student could make their own copy of a map by drawing it themselves but must not photocopy it.

5.69 What about examination questions?

Anything may be done for setting questions or answering them, so there are no restrictions in this area except that the questions must acknowledge the source of the material copies.

5.70 What about educational licensing schemes?

These apply to artistic works in a very limited way. See Section 10.

5.71 What is to be done for the classroom teacher who wants multiple copies of, say, a photograph for classroom use?

This is not permitted. However, each student might claim fair dealing to make their own copy for research or private study purposes.

5.72 Can a slide be included in, say, a film or video?

No. That is copying, just like any other form of copying.

5.73 Can an OHP transparency be made of a work for classroom use?

Not without infringing the copyright, although publishers have indicated that they would not regard this as an infringement if it were a single copy from an illustration, provided that the source was acknowledged.

5.74 Can slides or photographs be made of artistic works for classroom use or teaching?

Not without either infringing copyright or obtaining a licence.

5.75   Can copies be made of maps for classroom use?

Photocopies for classroom use cannot be made except under the licence of the copyright owner. Teachers and students may copy maps out of atlases by hand or through tracing paper, as this is not a reprographic process.

Library and archive copying

See also Section 4.

5.76   Can libraries and archives copy artistic works in their collections in the same way as printed materials?

No. The special provisions for library and archive copying do not apply to artistic works at all.

5.77   What is to be done for a reader who wants a copy of a photograph?

Readers may borrow the item and copy it for themselves if they think that would be fair, but the librarian is not allowed to copy it on behalf of readers. However, as fair dealing is not defined in law, it might be possible to argue that the librarian can copy for users under fair dealing provisions, provided they are certain that multiple copies have not been supplied.

5.78   What about copying maps for users?

Under copyright law this is not permitted. Users may make their own copies under fair dealing arrangements. But see Section 10 with regard to Ordnance Survey.

5.79   What about licences issued by publishers such as Ordnance Survey?

These are really a contract between the library and the copyright owner, who is allowing the library to do certain things that the law does not permit. As owner of the copyright, Ordnance Survey (or any other publisher) is entitled to do anything it wishes with its property! Failure to observe the conditions of such a licence is a breach of contract as well as an infringement of copyright. See also Section 10.

5.80 **Supposing an article in a periodical is accompanied by a photograph?**

This can safely be copied, as the Act makes it clear that accompanying materials can be legitimately copied, whether or not they are artistic works as such. But the photograph cannot be copied by itself – only as part of the article.

5.81 **Are libraries allowed to supply copies of artistic works through interlibrary copying?**

No.

5.82 **What if a library or archive has lost its copy of an artistic work? Can a replacement be obtained from another library or archive?**

No. Copying for preservation or replacement is restricted to literary, dramatic or musical works.

5.83 **Can artistic works be copied as a condition of export?**

Like literary works, an article of cultural or historical importance may be copied if a condition of the export is that a copy be made and deposited in an appropriate library or archive.

5.84 **What about material open for public inspection?**

No specific mention is made, with regard to material open to public inspection, of artistic works. For maps, however, see paragraph 4.321.

5.85 **Can artistic works be copied for public administration purposes?**

Yes, the same wide allowances apply to artistic works as to literary works.

5.86 **Do the rules for visually impaired people apply to artistic works?**

Yes, just like literary, dramatic and musical works. See paragraphs 4.328 and following.

Section 6
Sound recordings and performers' rights

Definition

6.1 **What is the definition of a sound recording?**

The definition of a sound recording is not limited in any way by format. It is any form of recording of sounds from which sounds may be reproduced. So it includes wax cylinders, vinyl discs, audio cassettes, compact discs and DVDs. It also includes sounds recorded and stored in digital form, from which sounds can be reproduced.

6.2 **Do the sounds have to be human voices or produced by musical instruments?**

No. The sounds could be of birdsong, or a steam train, for example.

Authorship

6.3 **Who is the author of a sound recording?**

The producer.

6.4 **Who counts as the producer?**

This term is defined as the 'person by whom the arrangements necessary for the making of the sound recording are made'.

6.5 **Does the producer of a sound recording enjoy moral rights?**

No (in a word!).

Ownership of copyright

6.6 **Who owns the copyright in a sound recording?**

It is owned by the recording company that produced the physical carrier of the recording if it is a commercial recording. If it is produced privately by an individual, then the individual will own the copyright. See also paragraph 3.19 for unpublished materials bequeathed to archives and libraries.

6.7   Who owns copyright in the content of a sound recording?

It is very important to distinguish between the copyright in the sound recording and the copyright in the material recorded.

Examples: A recording of a song by the Beatles will have all sorts of copyrights – the song, the music, the arrangement and the performance. In addition, there is a copyright in the actual sound recording, which is quite separate. Similarly, an interview for an oral history project will have a copyright in what the person said, which will belong to the person interviewed. There will also be a copyright in the recording made of that interview, which will be owned by the person who made the arrangements for making the recording. Again, a recording of Beethoven's Fifth Symphony will have a copyright in the recording, although there is no longer any copyright in the music as such. (This is important outside libraries as the law says it is not an infringement of the copyright in a sound recording to play it in organizations such as youth clubs. This applies only to the recording and not to the music or words of the recording.)

6.8   Who owns the copyright in an interview?

This is important for oral history and similar archives. The speaker owns the copyright in what is said, but there is no copyright in the material until it has been recorded. Once it has been recorded the speaker owns the copyright in what has been said, but the person making the recording owns the copyright in the sound recording as such. If the interview is transcribed, then the person making the transcription may also be entitled to copyright in the transcription.

6.9   Is it necessary to get permission to make such recordings for archives?

It is advisable to obtain the permission of the speaker when the recording is made. Such permission should stipulate for what purposes the recording will be used, especially whether it may be used later by a radio programme or television station. See the Oral History Society website for more information. Go to www.oralhistory.org.uk and click on 'Ethics'.

Owner's rights

6.10   What rights does the copyright owner have?

Essentially, the owner has the same rights as for literary, dramatic, musical or artistic works. See paragraphs 4.28 and following.

Copying the work

6.11   Does copying include copying from one medium to another?

Yes. To make a copy of a DVD onto a tape is, of course, copying the work. Copying a CD to go onto an iPod actually makes two copies – one on your hard disc and one on the iPod, both of which are technically infringing copies.

6.12   Supposing the medium on which the work is stored is obsolete? Can copies be made onto a usable type of equipment?

Not without permission or infringing copyright.

Issuing copies to the public

6.13   Who has the right to issue copies to the public?

This is an exclusive right of the owner.

Playing the work to the public

6.14   Who has the right to play the work?

The owner has the exclusive right to play the work.

6.15   Does this mean that if a library has a collection of sound recordings and wishes to put on a public performance of them, this is not allowed?

This can be done either with non-copyright material (i.e. it is too old to be protected), or with material in which the library or archive holds the copyright, or if the library is covered by a Performing Rights Licence and a Phonographic Performance Ltd (PPL) licence. See Section 10 on licences.

6.16   Supposing the library or archive holds oral history recordings. Can these be played publicly?

Only if the library/archive owns the copyright in both the words spoken and the sound recording itself.

6.17   How can the library or archive obtain the copyright in the actual words spoken?

This is best done by way of an agreement with the interviewee at the time of the interview. Failure to do this could lead to infringement of the speaker's copyright.

6.18   If the library has a collection of sound recordings, can they be played on the library's premises?

They can be played for private listening in carrels or somewhere similar, provided that not more than one person has access to the same recording at the same time, as this could be considered a public performance. Otherwise they can be played only if the library (or the library authority) has Performing Right Society and Phonographic Performance Ltd licences (see Section 10) which cover that building. Outside these limitations, public playing of copyright material is an infringement. Check with the administration to see if the library is covered by such a licence. This also applies to films, videos, television broadcasts and radio.

6.19   What about material available on the internet in libraries?

As at October 2009, this is a matter of dispute. The PRS is claiming that making music available to users of public libraries is causing it to be broadcast, even if it is listened to by one person at a time. Check the latest situation with CILIP or your local authority or university administration.

Communicating the work to the public by electronic means
6.20   Who has the right to communicate the work to the public by electronic means?

This is an exclusive right of the copyright owner.

6.21   Presumably libraries and archives do not have to worry about restrictions on broadcasting?

Not true. There is an increasing interest in local studies and live comments from the past, as well as folk music and recent broadcast interviews. Where this material has been prepared, recorded or given to the library or archive, it may well be in demand from local or national broadcasting stations. To allow it to be used in this way is an infringement, unless the original owner gave express permission when the recording was made.

Adaptation

6.22   Who has the right of adaptation?

This is an exclusive right of the owner. Transforming something from tape to CD is an infringement, as is copying a CD onto a PC and then transferring it to an iPod.

Lending and rental

6.23   If this right is an exclusive right of the owner, does this mean that lending services for audio materials are not allowed?

Basically, yes. Sound recordings may not be rented to the public without the copyright owner's permission. They can be lent by prescribed libraries (see paragraphs 4.256–4.264) provided the fee charged only covers the cost of administration, but they cannot be lent by public libraries without a licence of some kind. See Section 10.

6.24   Supposing a work is held by a library in both printed form and as, say, an audiocassette. What is the position then?

This causes an anomaly. The printed book may be subject to Public Lending Right but the audiocassette is controlled by the licensing scheme offered by the producers of audio materials, probably through the BPI (British Phonographic Industry) licence. There is a further anomaly, in that the money for the Public Lending Right royalty comes from the government and goes to the author; any money which may be generated by the audio licensing scheme (if there is one) is paid by the library and will probably go to the producer of the cassette.

6.25   Does this mean that libraries may no longer lend records?

Not altogether. In the first place, this restriction applies only to material acquired on or after 1 August, 1989. Second, there are special agreements with the production industries to allow lending facilities under specified terms. It is best to check the conditions of purchase of particular materials in the library (see also Section 10).

6.26   Why are public libraries excluded?

Because the Copyright Act stipulates that lending by public libraries of these materials is an infringement. Furthermore, the regulations on lending prohibit public libraries from lending material not covered by the Public Lending Right scheme.

6.27   Supposing there is no licensing scheme available?

The Secretary of State has the power to implement a scheme, subject to appropriate payment as determined by the Copyright Tribunal if necessary.

6.28   What about the rights that performers such as singers or instrumentalists have in sound recordings?

If it is allowed to lend the sound recording, then no rights of performers are infringed by that act of lending.

Publication right

6.29   Does publication right apply to sound recordings?

No.

Duration of copyright

6.30   How long does copyright in a sound recording last?

Essentially, 50 years from the end of the year in which it was made, but if it was released during that period or played in public or communicated to the public, then the 50-year period starts all over again. Note that, as at Summer 2009, there were proposals in the European Parliament to change the length of copyright protection to 70 years.

6.31   Do sound recordings have extended and revived copyright?

No. Duration of sound recordings is not linked to a human being, so the period is not extended, as for some other works.

Fair dealing

6.32   Is there fair dealing in sound recordings?

Only for very restricted purposes. See the individual headings below.

Research for a non-commercial purpose

6.33   There is no fair dealing in sound recordings for the purposes of research for a non-commercial use.

Private study

6.34   There is no fair dealing in sound recordings for the purposes of private study.

6.35   **What can be done for a student who needs a copy of a sound recording for study purposes?**

There is no legal way that such a copy can be provided, except for folksongs. See paragraph 6.41. The only thing to do is to obtain permission from the copyright owner.

Reporting current events

6.36   **Can sound recordings be used for reporting current events?**

Yes. Short extracts from appropriate recordings can be used for news items and there is no need to acknowledge their source.

Criticism and review

6.37   **Can sound recordings be used for criticism or review?**

Yes, so long as the source is acknowledged. So a broadcast which includes short extracts from sound recordings to provide comment on the work of a singer or composer is allowed.

Library and archive copying

6.38   **Can libraries and archives copy sound recordings?**

No. The provisions for copying in libraries and archives are for literary, dramatic and musical works only. Remember, a 'musical work' is the score as written or printed, not a sound recording of it!

6.39 Can a library or archive copy sound recordings for preservation purposes?

Unfortunately, no. Again, these allowances are for literary, dramatic or musical works only. (But see paragraphs 12.6–12.7 on changes to legal deposit.)

6.40 What can be done if a record or tape is deteriorating rapidly and will be lost if it is not copied?

Legally, nothing if it is still in copyright. If the owner can be traced, permission can be sought, but otherwise the library or archive may take a risk and produce a substitute copy. It is a matter of fine judgement whether the original copyright owner would take action if this were discovered.

6.41 What happens if someone wishes to record a folksong for an archive?

There are special rules for this. In the first place the song must be of unknown authorship and be unpublished. In other words, a real, original folksong. If this really is the case, then a recording can be made, so long as the performer does not prohibit this.

6.42 Can the recording be kept in any local history archive?

Not legally. Only certain designated archives can maintain collections of these items.

6.43 Which archives are these?

There are quite a number of them but they are all national in character. There is a complete list in SI 89/1012.

6.44 Can copies be made from these recordings?

Yes, provided that the archivist is satisfied that they are for research for a non-commercial purpose or private study only, and not more than one copy is supplied to any one person.

6.45 Is there the usual requirement that they must be paid for?

Surprisingly, no. No mention is made of payment.

6.46 Can copies be made for other archives?

Not under copyright law. The archives may have other agreements with production companies which allow this.

Other restrictions

Educational use

6.47   Is copying for educational purposes allowed?

Only in two specific cases (and one is very specific indeed). Copying for examinations is allowed (see paragraphs 4.171 and following) and copying for the purposes of giving instruction in the making of films or film soundtracks is allowed, provided it is done by the person giving the instruction and the purpose is non-commercial.

6.48   What about using sound recordings in the classroom?

If a sound recording is played in the classroom entirely for the purposes of instruction and only students and staff are present, this is not considered a public performance and is allowed. However, if the playing is for entertainment (end-of-term relaxation, some kind of club or just rainy playtime), then this is not allowed except under licence.

Copying as a condition of export

6.49   Do the special arrangements for copying materials of historic or cultural importance before export apply to sound recordings?

Yes. If the condition of export is that a copy is made and deposited in a library or archive, then this is not an infringement and the library or archive can make the copy, or receive the copy made elsewhere.

Material open to public inspection

6.50   Do the special conditions about copying such material apply to sound recordings?

It is not very likely that this would arise, but the appropriate person may make copies, either for use by persons who cannot exercise their statutory rights by consulting the material in person, or if the material contains information of general scientific, technical commercial or economic interest. Copies may not be made for persons consulting it in person.

Public administration

6.51 **Can sound recordings be copied for judicial proceedings, Parliamentary proceedings and statutory inquiries, as in the case of literary works?**

Yes. There is no restriction in these cases.

Rights in performances

6.52 **What are rights in performances?**

Anyone who performs a work in any of the defined categories enjoys the right to give consent to the using or copying of that performance.

6.53 **What are the categories of work which attract rights in performances?**

They are listed as:

- dramatic performance including dance or mime
- musical performance
- reading or recitation of a literary work
- a variety act.

6.54 **If someone recites a poem or makes a speech in an extempore fashion, without any written text or notes, is this a performance?**

No, and they do not enjoy any rights in it unless someone recorded it, in which case it becomes a literary work because it has been recorded (see paragraph 2.8). They do not enjoy any rights otherwise, because the recitation or reading must be of a literary work which, by definition, must already exist.

6.55 **What if the work performed is out of copyright?**

That makes no difference. A performance of one of Shakespeare's plays attracts rights for those who perform it because they are performing a literary work and it is their performance which is protected, not Shakespeare.

6.56 **What rights do performers have?**

Essentially, the same as copyright owners, namely giving their consent to:

- copying a recording of their performance
- issuing copies of the recording to the public
- lending or renting recordings of the performance
- making the performance available to the public by electronic means.

6.57 How long do these rights last?

As at Summer 2009 they last for 50 years from the end of the year in which the performance took place, or, if a recording of that performance is released during that period, then 50 years from the release of that recording. Note that this period is under review by the European Commission and may change. This is linked to proposed changes in the length of copyright in sound recordings. Note that the same rules apply to performances in relation to EEA and non-EEA countries as other works. See paragraphs 4.101 and following.

Section 7
Films, videos and DVDs

Definition

7.1 **What is the definition of a film?**

The definition of a film includes anything from which a moving image can by any means be produced. This covers film of all kinds, video, DVD and any other new technologies which produce moving images. Presumably it would also cover devices such as 'What the butler saw' too! Despite its name, a microfilm is not a film but a photograph!

Note that until July 1957 (when the 1956 Act came into force) films were protected only as a series of photographs.

Authorship

7.2 **Who is the author of a film?**

The producer and the principal director. Note that it is presumed that all films have both producers and principal directors and therefore all films are treated as having joint authorship unless these two functions are performed by the same person. Note that this applies only to films made on or after 1 July 1994. Before that date the author is defined simply as 'the person responsible for making the arrangements necessary for making the film'.

7.3 **Do the authors of films enjoy moral rights?**

Yes, the producer and principal director both enjoy moral rights in the same way as authors of literary works. See Section 3.

Ownership of copyright

7.4 **Who owns the copyright in a film?**

See paragraphs 3.8 and following on ownership for more detailed information.

Ownership of many rights in a film will depend on the contracts between the various people who made the film. Remember that the film will have many copyright elements.

Example: A filmed TV interview with a songwriter contains several performances of the songwriter's songs and an extract of a film containing performance of some of these songs. The songwriter may own the copyright in his or her words in the interview and the words and music of the songs; the person making the TV programme will own the copyright in the programme as a whole and the film maker will own some elements at least of the copyright in the extract of the film included in the programme.

However, if the film is made by a private person, then that person will own the copyright in the film. See also paragraphs 3.18–19 for unpublished materials bequeathed to archives and libraries.

7.5   Are the rules for extended and revived copyright the same (see paragraphs 3.25–26)?

Not quite. The extended copyright will be owned by the person who owned the copyright on 31 December 1995 but the revived copyright in the film will be owned by the principal director or his/her personal representative. But they will not own any revived copyright in the various elements of the film, such as the screenplay and music, and will need to negotiate with the owners of the copyright of these elements, if they are still in copyright, for rights to exploit the revived copyright in the film as a whole.

Owner's rights

7.6   What rights does the copyright owner have?

The owner has the same rights as for literary, dramatic and musical works detailed below.

Copying films

7.7   Does this include copying from one medium to another?

Yes. To make a copy of, say, a film to a DVD is copying the work.

7.8   **Supposing the medium on which the work is stored is obsolete? Can copies be made onto a usable type of medium?**

Not without the permission of the copyright owner.

7.9   *Issuing copies to the public*

This is an exclusive right of the owner.

7.10   *Performing the work*

The owner has the exclusive right to show the work in public.

For other matters relating to performance of a work see paragraphs 4.42 and following and 6.14 and following, since the same basic rules apply and the same problems arise.

7.11   *Communicating the work to the public*

See paragraph 4.51 and following for details.

7.12   *Adaptation*

The owner has the exclusive right to adapt the work.

Lending and rental

7.13   **If this right is an exclusive right of the owner, does this mean that lending services for video and DVD materials are not allowed?**

No. Lending by prescribed libraries (other than public libraries) is allowed, provided that any charges made cover no more than the administrative costs of making the loan.

7.14   **Does this mean that public libraries may no longer lend videos?**

Not altogether. In the first place, this restriction applies only to material acquired on or after 1 August 1989. Second, there may well be special agreements with the production industries to allow rental/lending facilities under agreed terms. It is best either to check the conditions of purchase of particular materials in the library or to seek advice on the latest situation from CILIP (see Appendix 1).

7.15   **Why are public libraries excluded?**

Because public libraries may lend only materials which (a) were purchased before

December 1996 or (b) are covered by the Public Lending Right scheme or (c) are covered by special agreements with the industry at large or with specific production companies or their agents.

7.16   Supposing there is no lending scheme available?

The Secretary of State has the power to implement a scheme, subject to appropriate payment as determined by the Copyright Tribunal if necessary.

7.17   What about shops that rent out DVDs and videos?

They do this by paying the distributor a licence fee and thus with their agreement.

7.18   What about the rights that performers such as singers or instrumentalists have in films or videos?

If it is allowed to lend the film or video, then no rights of performers are infringed by that act of lending.

Publication right

7.19   Are films subject to publication right?

Yes, in the same way as literary, dramatic and musical works. See paragraphs 4.91 and following.

Duration of copyright

7.20   Do the rules about works originating in the EEA (see paragraph 4.101) also apply?

Yes, the rules in this area are the same. To avoid repetition, the 70-year rule is marked with a * to remind you that the EEA/non-EEA rules apply.

7.21   How long does the copyright in a film last?

Copyright in a film lasts for 70* years from the end of the year in which the last of the following died:

- the principal director
- the author of the screenplay
- the author of the dialogue
- the composer of music specially created for and used in the film.

7.22   **It is not always easy to find out who all these people are or when they died. What can be done then?**

When the identity of at least one of them is known, then copyright expires as in paragraphs 4.16–4.17.

7.23   **What if the identity of none of them can be found?**

Then copyright expires 70* years from the end of the year in which the film was made, unless, during that time, it was made available to the public.

7.24   **What happens if it was made available to the public?**

Then copyright runs for 70* years from the end of the year in which that took place.

7.25   **Is 'made available to the public' the same as 'published'?**

Not quite. In the context of a film it means being shown in public or included in a broadcast or cable television programme.

7.26   **Sometimes nobody in particular is responsible for making a film. What happens about copyright then?**

If it is not possible to say that anyone took on the distinctive responsibilities listed in paragraph 7.21, then none of these rules applies and copyright expires 50 years from the end of the year in which the film was made.

7.27   **Does the soundtrack of a film count as a sound recording or a film?**

The soundtrack of a film counts as part of the film and therefore gets the length of protection of the film, but there can also be rights in it as a sound recording in its own right.

Fair dealing

7.28   **Is there fair dealing in films?**

There is fair dealing in film, DVD or video only for the specific cases mentioned below.

7.29 *Research for a non-commercial purpose or private study*

There is no fair dealing in films or videos for research for a non-commercial purpose or private study.

7.30 *Reporting current events*

This applies to films, DVDs, etc. See paragraphs 4.158 and following.

7.31 *Criticism and review*

This applies to films, DVDs, etc. See paragraphs 4.153 and following.

Library and archive copying

7.32 **Can libraries or archives copy films or videos in their collections?**

In general, no. The special provisions for library and archive copying apply only to literary, dramatic or musical works, but not to other works. Copying for preservation or transferring from one medium to another are also not allowed.

7.33 **What is to be done for a researcher who needs a copy of part of a film or video?**

The copy cannot be supplied unless the copyright in the material is owned by the library or archive or the original copyright owner has given permission for copies to be made.

7.34 **Can copies be made for other archives?**

Not under copyright law. The library or archives may have other agreements with production companies which allow this.

Other restrictions

Educational use

7.35 **Can films be copied for classroom use?**

No. But there is an exception for training in the making of films or film soundtracks, and then only by the teacher or student themselves and also for a non-commercial purpose.

7.36 **What about using films in the classroom?**

If a film or video is shown in the classroom of an educational establishment entirely for the purposes of instruction and only students and staff are present, this is not considered a public performance and is allowed. Use for recreational purposes (see paragraphs 6.48 and 10.37) is not permitted except with a licence.

Copying as a condition of export

7.37 Can films be copied as a condition of export?

Yes. See paragraph 4.308.

Public administration

7.38 Can films be copied for public administration?

Yes. See paragraphs 4.309 and following.

Material open to public inspection

7.39 Can films that are open to public inspection be copied?

Yes. See paragraphs 4.314 and following.

Multimedia

7.40 If a publication contains material in several different forms, such as a booklet, computer program and DVD, how is the copyright worked out?

The copyright will subsist separately in each item and the rules for that format will apply. So the copyright in the entire package could run out at several different times. In that sense, it is no different from a periodical issue. It may also be a database (see Section 9).

7.41 Who is the author of a mixed-media package?

The rules for ownership and authorship are the same as for each of the components. However, the publisher will almost certainly own copyright in the format of the whole package.

7.42 Presumably performers have rights in films, just as in sound recordings?

Yes. See paragraphs 6.56–6.57 for details of performers' rights.

Section 8
Broadcasts

Most matters relating to broadcasts, from a library and archive point of view, are dealt with under either 'sound recordings' or 'films'.

Definition

8.1 What is the definition of a broadcast?

The definition of a broadcast is 'an electronic transmission of visual images, sounds or other information which is transmitted for simultaneous reception by members of the public and is capable of lawfully being received by them or is transmitted at a time determined solely by the person making the transmission for presentation to members of the public'.

8.2 Some people used to say that websites were broadcasting. Is this still true?

No. The law specifically states that any internet transmission is excluded from the definition of a broadcast unless: it is a transmission taking place simultaneously on the internet and by other means; it is a concurrent transmission of a live event; or it is a transmission of recorded moving images or sounds forming part of a programme service offered by the person responsible for making the transmission, and is part of a service transmitted at scheduled times determined by that person. This is rather wordy, so some examples may help. A film is being shown on TV and simultaneously can be watched on your PC via the internet; a horse race can be watched on both TV and via the internet on your PC; a website is designed so that you can view/listen to items on it only at times fixed by the website manager. In all these cases transmission is considered as a broadcast, not internet transmission. As mentioned in Section 4, in a nutshell, broadcasting takes precedence over internet transmission when determining the status of a transmitted work.

8.3 **So are cable programme services included?**

Yes, a cable programme service now fits the definition of a broadcast, although it used to be a separate class of material.

Authorship

8.4 **Who is the author of a broadcast?**

Essentially, it is the person who transmits the programme, if that person has any responsibility for its contents.

8.5 **Does the author enjoy moral rights?**

Once again, in a word, no!

Ownership of copyright

8.6 **Who owns the copyright in a broadcast?**

Usually the person who transmits the programme.

8.7 **What about a broadcast which includes a record or a film?**

There are separate copyrights in the broadcast and in the sound recording included in it. In the same way, a television programme which includes a film has separate copyrights in the television transmission and in the film in the programme. This is similar to typographical copyright.

8.8 **As broadcasts often come from many different countries, which one is regarded as the original?**

The country where the uninterrupted signal started is regarded as the country of origin.

8.9 **Supposing it is a satellite broadcast?**

Legislation makes it clear that where the satellite is merely a retransmission point it has no significance in determining where the broadcast came from.

Owners' rights

8.10 **What rights do owners of copyright in broadcasts have?**

Owners have the same rights as in literary, etc. works. See Section 3.

Communicating the work to the public

8.11 How does the right of communicating the work to the public fit in?

By making a broadcast of any work, not only is a broadcast created, but the right of communicating the work to the public is also brought into play. So to broadcast anything requires the consent of the copyright owner. Similarly, putting anything on the internet is also an act requiring the permission of the copyright owner.

Lending and rental

8.12 How is lending and rental relevant to broadcasts?

Although this may not seem relevant to broadcasts, copies of broadcasts which may be lent or rented must be considered as copies of those broadcasts, even though they also constitute sound recordings or films. In educational establishments lending of recordings made under Educational Recording Agency (ERA) and Open University (OU) licences may be restricted. Copies made under the legislation must not be transmitted to persons outside the establishment, so this may prevent copies of broadcasts being lent to students who might then take them home or elsewhere off the premises. The law is not clear on this point.

Publication right

8.13 Is publication right relevant to broadcasts?

This is not relevant to broadcasts.

Duration of copyright

8.14 When does the copyright in a broadcast expire?

Copyright in a broadcast expires 50 years after the year when the broadcast was made or the programme was included in a cable television service.

8.15 What about repeats?

The fact that a programme was repeated does not extend or renew the copyright.

Fair dealing

8.16   Is there fair dealing in broadcasts?

Fair dealing in broadcasts is allowed for reporting current events and for criticism and review. The source of the broadcast must be acknowledged where possible.

8.17   Supposing I want to record something because I am out and will miss it or it clashes with another programme I want to watch/hear?

Copying from the radio or television for personal use to listen or view at a more convenient time is allowed, provided that the copy is used only for private purposes and the copying is done on your own domestic premises. This is technically called 'time-shifting'.

8.18   Supposing I ask friends round to watch the recording?

Provided they were friends or relations and you did not make any charge, this would be legal.

8.19   Supposing I just want to take a photo of a TV broadcast, perhaps because it has someone I know on it?

A single copy of an image from a broadcast for private and domestic use is allowed, but it must not be further copied.

Educational copying

8.20   Can broadcasts be copied for classroom use, too?

This must be done either with the appropriate licence or under the law as described below. Such licences are now generally available for educational establishments. See Section 10. One exception is for training in the making of films or film soundtracks and then only by the teacher or student themselves. But broadcasts can be played or viewed by a class as they are transmitted.

8.21   Are all broadcasts licensed?

No. The ERA licenses educational establishments to copy broadcasts from BBC, ITV and Channel 5, and the OU issues licences for its own broadcasts. The licences do not cover material from other cable or satellite broadcasts or material broadcast from outside the UK. These broadcasts may be freely recorded, as the law states that, where no licence is offered, recording is legitimate for educational use.

8.22 **Are there any restrictions?**

If you copy under an ERA or OU licence you must observe the limits of that licence. Other copying is subject to the following conditions:

- the source of the broadcast must be acknowledged
- the educational purpose must be non-commercial
- the copy of the broadcast must not be transmitted to any person outside the premises of the establishment.

8.23 **Can recordings of these broadcasts be lent or transmitted to students?**

This will depend on the location of the student to whom the recording is transmitted (which presumably includes lending). Such broadcasts must not be transmitted to people off the premises, which would include distance learning students and many working in virtual learning environments (VLEs) or managed learning environments (MLEs). So lending a copy to a student may mean that it is taken off the premises which would have the same effect. But the term 'transmitted' is not defined.

8.24 **What about podcasts and similar services?**

Because these can be viewed at times chosen by the viewer they are not legally broadcasts and are outside the ERA licence and the scope of the exceptions under the law.

8.25 **Does this mean that organizations that are not considered educational can make off-air recordings?**

No. The provisions and the licences apply only to educational establishments.

Library and archive copying

8.26 **Can libraries and archives record off-air for their collections?**

This is permitted only for specified collections, which, as at Summer 2009, are British Film Institute, British Library, British Medical Association, British Music Information Centre, Imperial War Museum, Music Performance Research Centre, National Library of Wales and the Scottish Film Council.

8.27   Can other archives keep off-air recordings made for 'time shifting' purposes?

No. They must be kept and used by the person who made them for their own use. Only designated archives can retain material for archival purposes. Copies made under the ERA licences are a different matter and can be kept indefinitely. OU broadcasts usually have conditions relating to the length of time they are kept. Notification of this time limit, set by the OU, is attached to them.

8.28   Supposing someone's papers are deposited with an archive and these papers include copies of audiovisual materials such as off-air recordings. Can the archive keep these?

In theory, no. They are infringing copies because off-air recording can be done only for certain limited purposes and storing the copies in an archive is not one of them.

Section 9
Databases

Definition

9.1   What is the definition of a database?

A database is defined as 'a collection of works, data or other materials which: (a) are arranged in a systematic or methodical way and (b) are individually accessible by electronic or other means'.

9.2   Are databases protected by copyright?

Databases can certainly be subject to copyright but they are also subject to a quite separate database right.

9.3   Can a literary work also be a database?

Yes, it can. In order to be recognized as a literary work, a database will be eligible only if it is original (a vital test for copyright protection) and the selection of the contents and arrangement of the database constitute the author's own intellectual creation. In this case the database will acquire copyright protection.

9.4   Must a database be electronic to be protected?

Definitely not. The phrase 'other means' makes this quite clear.

Copyright and database right

9.5   Can a database be subject to both copyright and database right?

A database can be subject to both copyright and database right and it is very important to remember this when reading the following paragraphs.

9.6   What is the difference between copyright and database right?

Essentially, a database is subject to copyright if it is a work of personal intellectual activity; otherwise it does not attract copyright but does attract database right. If someone devotes their entire academic life to compiling an annotated bibliography on a particular subject with comments, evaluations and selection of materials, then this would attract copyright. A monthly bibliography on the same subject produced by library staff without any real selective judgement and with no one author would merely be a database.

9.7   Are all databases protected by database right?

All modern ones will be, but some databases which are quite old (before 1983) will qualify only for copyright under the term 'compilation' (see paragraph 9.19 below for exact details and paragraph 4.107 for compilations).

9.8   How does something qualify for database right?

To qualify for database right the contents of the database must have been assembled as the result of substantial investment in obtaining, verifying or presenting the contents.

9.9   Does investment just mean money?

No. Investment specifically includes financial, human or technical resources.

9.10   Does 'obtain' mean you must get the data from somewhere else?

Yes, and this is a vital point about databases. It has been ruled that in order to claim database right you must obtain the data. Obtaining means that it already exists. Anyone who creates a database from scratch cannot claim database right, only copyright.

Example: Someone makes a list of retail outlets in a town (see paragraph 9.30). This forms a database and qualifies because someone has obtained the data about the shops. Someone else plans a calendar of events for the village choral society. This cannot be a database because they did not obtain the data but created it and, until they chose the events, that data did not exist.

9.11   If the database is made up of material which is not copyright, is the database still protected?

Yes, if it qualifies as a database. The copyright status of the content of a database is irrelevant. It is the construction of the database that is the key question.

9.12   So can anyone use non-copyright material that is included in a database?

Yes, provided they do not extract a substantial part of the database.

9.13   Supposing out-of-copyright material is collected from a number of databases, as permitted, and then organized into a new database. Does this also qualify for database right?

Yes, because the data has been obtained and then verified and presented.

Authorship

9.14   Who is the author of a database?

Apart from the fairly rare occasion when a database has a personal author (see paragraph 4.23), the author is defined as the maker of the database. The maker of a database is the person who takes the initiative in obtaining, verifying or presenting the contents of the database and assumes the risk of investing in those actions and therefore obtains the database right. Makers cannot qualify for this right unless they are individuals with EEA nationality or companies/organizations incorporated within the EEA or partnerships or unincorporated bodies formed under the law of an EEA state.

9.15   Are there moral rights in databases?

There are no moral rights in databases unless they are the creation of an individual person, when the usual rules about derogatory treatment would apply.

Ownership of copyright and database right

9.16   Who is the owner of database right?

Where copyright subsists, the copyright rules apply (see Section 3). Ownership of database right belongs to the maker of the database, although the usual rules about ownership of works made as part of employment or for the Crown apply (paragraphs 3.14 and 3.27–3.28).

Duration of copyright and database right

9.17   How long do the rights in databases last?

When a database attracts copyright protection the usual rules for duration of copyright for literary works apply (see paragraphs 4.99 and following). When database right applies this lasts for 15 years from the end of the year in which the database was completed. If, during that time, it is made available to the public, then the 15-year term runs from the end of the year in which the database was made available.

9.18   But databases are constantly being updated. What happens to the length of protection then?

If substantial changes, including accumulation of data, additions or deletions, take place such that the updated database would be considered the subject of substantial new investment, then the 15-year period will begin again. In other words, where a database is frequently being updated it will remain protected by database right for 15 years after the final changes have been made.

9.19   What about old databases?

Where a database was completed after 1 January 1983 and the database right began to operate when the regulations came into force, then that database obtains database right until 31 December 2012.

9.20   What about databases which already exist but which would not qualify for copyright under the new rules?

If the database was made before 27 March 1996 and was copyright immediately before the regulations came into force, then it remains in copyright under the usual rules for copyright duration.

Owners' rights

9.21   What rights does the owner of copyright and database right enjoy?

The rights of database right owners are defined in a different way from those of a copyright owner.

9.22   What rights does the owner of database right have?

The owner of database right has the right to prevent the extraction or re-utilization of all or a substantial part of the contents of the database.

9.23   **What precisely does 'extraction' mean?**

The word 'extraction' is defined as 'permanent or temporary transfer of the contents to another medium by any means or in any form'.

9.24   **Does this mean that nothing can ever be taken from a database?**

No. A user is allowed to extract small amounts of data provided that the amount taken is insubstantial.

9.25   **What counts as insubstantial?**

This is not defined, but in deciding if the amount taken is substantial or not, quality and quantity are both factors, separately and together. So it is possible to take a small quantity but still infringe the database right because of the quality of what has been taken. The reverse is also true.

Example: It might be considered that three or four entries from different parts of the 'white' telephone pages is not substantial but to take the addresses of all four companies listed in the Yellow Pages under a highly specific classification could be substantial. In addition, the courts have judged that a substantial part of a database must be so large that it would be in competition with the original database from which it was taken. So this might be a very large amount.

9.26   **Supposing someone copies an insubstantial amount one day and then does the same a few days later. Is this allowed?**

No. The law has spotted this cunning ploy. It specifies that systematic extraction of insubstantial parts of a database may amount to extraction of substantial amounts. In other words, extractions done at different times must be seen as cumulative.

9.27   **What about 're-utilization'? Does this stop me using any information?**

No. 'Re-utilization' is defined as 'making the contents available to the public by any means'. Re-utilization is dealt with under 'Fair dealing'.

9.28   **Surely this is making facts subject to copyright?**

Not really. Copyright and the other rights associated with it refer to using someone else's property. Imagine someone has compiled a list of ice-cream makers in East Coast resorts. There is nothing to stop someone else compiling their own list and issuing this as a free or commercial product, provided they have compiled it from scratch and not used the other person's list. The idea behind database right is to give some protection to the person who invested in putting the data together in the first place, not to give them exclusive control over those facts but over the way those facts have been assembled and made available.

9.29 What about other rights such as copying, issuing to the public and so on?

These are really covered by the right to prevent extraction and re-utilization. If you cannot extract, then you cannot do any of the things a copyright owner would have the exclusive right to do anyway. Other rights, such as performance, publication right or making available right would not apply to databases.

Fair dealing

9.30 Are databases subject to fair dealing in the same way as literary works?

Yes, but with an important difference. Where a database is copyright, then it is subject to fair dealing for research for a non-commercial purpose or private study, provided the source is indicated. Where the database is subject only to database right then the following rules apply.

First, if you need to use a substantial part of the database, you can do this provided that it is for non-commercial research or private study. So you can certainly look up the addresses of the five or six ice-cream manufacturers in Bridlington and Scarborough and write them down for your own use but this information cannot be issued to the public in the form of a trade directory, database or in any other way. Whether you need to write down on your piece of paper by the telephone the source of the information to comply with this rule seems highly unlikely! Second, if the amount taken is insubstantial and you are a lawful user of the database you can extract *and* re-utilize this information, but not use it and repackage it for publication or further use. But remember that insubstantial amounts may be very small amounts indeed!

9.31 Why is commercial research excluded?

The law is quite specific that *anything* done to a database for the purposes of research for a commercial purpose is not fair dealing with that database.

9.32   Is there a definition of 'commercial'?

No, but any use which will bring commercial benefit to an organization or individual would be considered as commercial.

9.33   What constitutes a lawful user?

A lawful user is someone who has a right to use the database. In a paper context this is anyone entitled to use the library where it is stored or any private owner of a database or anyone they permit to have access to it. In the electronic context it will be anyone who legitimately has a licence to use or be allowed to use the database.

9.34   Are users of library services lawful users?

This will depend on the licence the library has with the database owner. In electronic situations it is important to ensure that the library's licence includes as wide a range of users as possible so that nobody is excluded. For commercial companies lawful users may be a much more restricted group (e.g. company employees only, or even only those in the R&D department).

9.35   Some electronic databases come with very strict licences. Can these prevent any use of the database at all?

Not legally. The terms of any contract which aims to prevent a lawful user from extracting or re-utilizing insubstantial parts of the database will be considered null and void in law.

Educational copying

9.36   Can databases be copied for educational purposes?

Where a database is protected only by copyright then the usual rules apply. Where database right exists, then it is not infringed if a substantial part is extracted for the purposes of illustration for teaching or research and this is not done for any commercial purpose and the source is acknowledged.

9.37   Does this mean to illustrate research?

This is not at all clear. Whether 'illustration' belongs with teaching or 'teaching and research' is not stated. The words given are those from the law – only a judge may ever sort this out!

Library and archive copying

9.38 Can databases be made available through libraries?

Essentially, the answer is 'yes'. Certainly under a licence from the database owner this can be done, but it is essential to ensure that all legitimate users of the library are designated as 'lawful users', otherwise they do not have the right to use any of the material in the database. If the database is in paper format, problems of access do not arise in database right terms, but the issue of what users may copy will remain.

9.39 Can libraries copy parts of databases for users?

Where a database is copyright (only) then libraries may copy it as they can other library works (a reasonable proportion); however, library copying is not permitted for database right, so the ability of libraries to copy in this respect is limited to copying an insubstantial part.

Other restrictions

Adaptation

9.40 Supposing someone took a database, altered the way it was arranged and then re-issued it?

This is not allowed, as the law specifically defines adaptation as including arrangement or alteration of the version or translation.

Lending and rental

9.41 Presumably libraries cannot lend databases?

Yes, they can. It is easy to think that database = electronic database, but these rules apply to paper copies too. So, the lending of a database is not considered as extraction or re-utilization and is therefore allowed under the same conditions as literary works. Similarly, on-the-spot reference is permitted. However, public libraries cannot lend databases, as they are not covered by PLR.

Making copies available for public inspection

9.42 Can databases be made available for public inspection?

Similar rules to those for literary works apply to databases.

Public administration

9.43 Can databases be made available for the purpose of public administration?

Similar rules to those for literary works apply to databases.

Visually impaired people

9.44 Can databases be made available in alternative formats for VIPs?

Not under the current law, because this was introduced as a result of EU legislation which specifically excluded any changes to existing laws relating to databases. However, the industry guidelines on making materials available for VIPs are much more generous and do not exclude databases. Consult www.pls.org.uk for more details on industry guidelines in this area.

Section 10
Licensing schemes and licences

10.1 The situation relating to licensing schemes and licences is changing all the time. What is given in this section is simply an outline of the major schemes and licences, how they work and what benefits and limitations they bring. Details of individual licensing schemes need to be obtained from the relevant agency or organization. Addresses, including appropriate websites and addresses are given in Appendix 1. The outline information in this chapter is current as at Spring 2009.

10.2 What is the difference between a licensing scheme and a licence?

A licensing scheme is one which covers a defined range of works and is offered to a particular class of organization (government departments, academic institutions) and which anyone who is in the class named can join. A licence is more often an agreement between the copyright owner and an individual user. Its terms may be similar to a licensing scheme but are usually tailored to the specific needs of the user.

Licensing schemes
10.3 What is a licensing scheme?

Basically, it is a scheme which allows someone who is not the copyright owner to use copyright material beyond the limits of the law, with the permission of the copyright owner.

10.4 Who administers such schemes?

They are administered by different organizations, and these can change. They are briefly described in the following paragraphs. In addition, copyright owners can, and do, issue their own independent licences. These may be 'one-off' owners of copyright or large organizations such as the BBC or Ordnance Survey.

10.5   Are licensing schemes relevant to libraries?

Certainly, because any licence held by the organization which owns or administers the library may include copying done in the library or by library staff. But it is unusual for licensing schemes to be only for the library. The library is part of a larger organization which is licensed as a whole.

10.6   Do libraries have to abide by the rules of such licences?

Yes. They represent a contract between the licensing agency and the licensee.

10.7   What are the details of such schemes?

Each scheme will vary according to the type of material covered and the type of organization holding the licence. The terms and conditions of licences vary from one type of organization to another and from time to time, so anything said here about the terms of a licence should be checked with the licensing agency before a licence is considered. These notes are for general guidance only. Note too that a licence is a contract and the terms of the contract are what count in the end, not advice or comments in a general book on copyright, such as this one!

10.8   How do licences work with exceptions such as fair dealing, library privilege and education?

Essentially, the licence is there to permit copying or use beyond what the law permits, so a licence should not include clauses which prohibit the exercise of privileges granted by Parliament. But if it does, and these terms have been agreed, it appears that those privileges have been signed away.

10.9   What about copying publications from other countries?

The Copyright Licensing Agency (CLA) has agreements with a number of countries to collect royalties on behalf of copyright owners in those countries. An up-to-date list can be obtained from the CLA.

10.10   What are the major licensing agencies and schemes?

The brief descriptions below give a general idea of each agency and the type of licence it offers. Specific details should be obtained from the appropriate agency.

10.11   Copyright Licensing Agency

The CLA is owned jointly by the societies representing authors and publishers. The Copyright Licensing Agency is the largest agency that libraries will encounter.

It offers a range of licences to copy onto and from paper and can now offer licences for fax and scanning. Some licences currently offer the making of scanned copies and putting them onto a secure intranet site as well as copying and storing from electronic 'born digital' material, although this latter facility is optional for the publisher. Again, see the CLA website for details. The CLA also has an agreement with the Design and Artists Copyright Society (DACS), so the CLA can now offer a licence which includes the copying of artistic work embedded in text items as well.

10.12   Educational copying

The CLA licence allows one copy of one article from a periodical issue or 5% of a book or one chapter; one copy for each pupil in a class and one for the teacher, whether school, college or university. Libraries may also be allowed to make one copy of such material for the short-loan collection. Separate licences currently exist for LEA schools, independent schools, FE colleges and Higher Education Institutions (HEIs). As details vary, consult the CLA website for details.

10.13   Government departments

CLA licences are structured according to the needs of the department.

10.14   Industry and commerce

A model CLA licence was negotiated with the Confederation of British Industry (CBI) which it could recommend to its members (but could not negotiate for them). This is essentially a matrix consisting of the sector in which the company operates and the number of research staff they employ. A similar licence has been negotiated for legal firms with the Law Society. There is also a special licence for regulatory material required by the pharmaceutical industry. These licences often include scanning UK publications and putting the image onto a secure intranet site.

10.15   Other CLA licences

Other licences have been issued for the NHS, local authorities and learned societies. It is likely that licences will be available to all sectors in the near future.

10.16   Does the licence cover copying for visually impaired people?

The CLA licence includes the making of copies in large print, Braille and Moon, but not audio.

10.17 What about providing copies to people outside my organization?

The CLA currently (Summer 2009) offers three document delivery licences:

- Transactional Document Delivery Licence
- Low Volume Document Delivery Licence
- Sticker scheme.

10.18 What are the differences?

The *Transactional Document Delivery Licence* allows any library to provide copies of documents for commercial research. It is designed for libraries which deliver more than 100 copies a month for commercial research. Copyright fees are set individually by publishers. It is similar to the British Library scheme (see paragraph 4.252).

The *Low Volume Document Delivery Licence* is intended for libraries which deliver fewer than 100 copies a month for commercial purposes. The copyright fee is a flat fee.

The *sticker scheme* is intended for libraries which have walk-in users who are not employees or members of the institution: for example, anyone using a public library or a member of the general public using a university library. This scheme is also a flat-fee one. The library collects the fee from the user and passes it to the CLA with bibliographic details of the works covered and the CLA eventually raises an invoice for the amount collected. The user attaches a copy of the form to the photocopy to show it is legitimate.

10.19 Why can't an employee of a company with a CLA licence simply go into a public library and make a copy under the firm's licence?

The CLA licence only covers material, copies of which are owned by the organization holding the licence. So anything in the public library, of which the company did not own its own copy, could not be covered by the company's licence.

10.20 So why can't copies be made under the licence held by the local authority or university?

Because the CLA licence allows copying only by employees or consultants working for the organization holding the licence. So the reader in a public library or visitor to a university library cannot be covered by this licence.

10.21 **Many journals have details of payment to the Copyright Clearance Center in the USA printed on the bottom of the page. Must libraries pay these fees to CCC?**

Payment should be made only if copying is done beyond what UK law permits. The CLA currently acts as the agent for the CCC and it should be contacted in cases of doubt. The national copyright agencies work together to form an international network through which payments are transferred.

10.22 **Christian Copyright Licensing International**

CCLI offers a licence for the copying of both the words and music of many hymns. Licences are available for churches, schools and conference centres but the original work must be owned by the licensee. Borrowing copies from a library outside the licensed organization and then copying is not covered by the licence. The scheme is remarkable as the first to license copying of music of any kind.

10.23 **Newspaper Licensing Agency**

Unlike the CLA, the NLA is wholly owned by the newspaper publishing industry. The NLA offers a range of licences to different sectors. There is a standard copying licence, but separate terms. Currently the licence covers all national and the vast majority of regional newspapers as well as newspapers from a number of overseas publishers. Check the NLA website for specific details.

10.24 **What does the NLA licence allow?**

The NLA licence allows:

- photocopying, faxing and digital reproduction of press cuttings
- copying for internal management purposes
- copying for educational purposes
- in certain cases, copying to members and clients.

10.25 **Can someone with an NLA licence copy material in other libraries?**

Yes. Unlike the CLA licence, the NLA licence covers the copying of all the newspapers licensed, regardless of whether the licensee owns a copy of them or not.

10.26 Design and Artists Copyright Society

This licence is slightly different from others in that it legitimizes existing infringing collections of slides in educational establishments as well as licensing the making of new slides. Organizations joining declare their infringing collections and pay a one-off fee for them; there is then an annual licence fee based on the number of slides made. The scheme includes all artistic works as listed on the DACS website, including those published in books, and DACS offers an indemnity in the case of users being challenged. DACS also has an arrangement for licensing artistic works through the CLA licensing system. At present there is no digital copying scheme, partly because artists are highly sensitive to the manipulation of their work once it is in digital format.

10.27 Educational Recording Agency

The ERA offers a licence for educational establishments only for off-air recording of broadcasts (TV and radio) from the following:

- BBC television and radio
- ITV Network services (including ITV2 and ITV3)
- Channel 4 and E4
- Five television
- S4C.

As there is no licence for other cable or satellite broadcasting at present, these programmes may be freely recorded for educational purposes, unless the contract for receiving these services explicitly excludes recording for educational purposes, which some contracts do. Once recorded, a copy may be used for teaching and further copied within the terms of the licence. It may be kept in the library of the institution for which it was recorded. Licensed items must be labelled as such and may be lent only in exceptional circumstances, within the terms of the ERA licence. Recording does not have to be done on the premises – it could be done by a teacher or lecturer at home for subsequent use within the licensed premises. The ERA digital licence permits the streaming of broadcasts to eligible students, but only within the licensed premises.

10.28 Open University Educational Enterprises

The OUEE licence is clearly specific for OU output. Again, it is available only to educational establishments. Payment is according to the number of recordings kept for more than 30 days. Recordings kept for fewer than 30 days are not paid for but all recordings must be registered. As OU moves away from using TV as a method of communicating with students this licence is likely to become less significant.

10.29 HMSO

Government policy means that many documents published or controlled by HMSO may be freely copied. Most legislation and similar material, many official reports and documents can all be copied and reused. Single and multiple copies are allowed and documents may be included in other works (such as textbooks), and they can be included in websites and other publications. The Royal Coat of Arms may not be included as this has become a sort of Trademark or Guarantee of integrity. In addition, material classed as Public Records (see paragraph 4.324) may be freely copied, republished, included in books and journal articles, used as the basis for making a broadcast or film, indexed or translated without payment of any fee. The source of the document must be acknowledged and its integrity respected and the institution holding the document may charge the fees necessary to cover the costs of providing the document. As this is a rapidly changing area, it is best to consult the HMSO website for the latest guidance. See www.opsi.gov.uk/advice/crown-copyright/copyright-guidance/index.

10.30 Ordnance Survey

Because maps are artistic works, copying of these by libraries is not permitted although individuals may claim fair dealing. The OS has introduced a wide range of licences for education, local authorities, commerce and business, legal procedures and planning permissions. They are very detailed and liable to quite radical change from time to time and it would be misleading to describe them all here. The most important one for the general public and public libraries is that OS allows a library to supply copies, or a member of the public to make copies, up to the following limits: 4 copies may be made, provided that they are from a single map and that no more than 625 cm^2 (A4 size) is made and this is at the original size – no enlargements are allowed. There are separate schemes for local authorities and planning applications and libraries are advised not to get involved in copying for these purposes, as they may not be aware of the finer points of the agreement. Details of educational, commercial and other types of licence should be obtained from OS direct.

10.31 British Standards Institution

BSI issues special licences for classroom use. In the case of Standards in public collections, BSI has stated that it considers that up to 10% of a Standard can be copied without infringement.

10.32 British Library Document Supply Centre

The British Library Document Supply Centre (BLDSC) holds a licence from the CLA which allows it to make copies beyond the limits of the provisions for libraries, in return for the payment of royalties set by the copyright owners. These royalties are collected in full from the requester of the documents. Basically, when a copy is supplied through this service a number of the limitations imposed by the law no longer apply. Copies can be supplied to both individuals and libraries and are increasingly in electronic form. Full details of the copyright restrictions on copies from the British Library can be obtained from marketing@bl.uk. But it is particularly important to note that copies may not be further copied except under the strict terms of any CLA licence held by the organization receiving the copies.

10.33 British Phonographic Industry

Libraries may not lend sound recordings except under licence, and such a licence has been negotiated by CILIP with the BPI for public libraries (only). This is based on a combination of the number of copies of any one work held at any one service point and a 'holdback' period for new releases, when they will not be lent. There is no licence fee.

10.34 Performing Right Society

The PRS is one of the oldest licensing societies in the world. It licenses all public performances of music, whether these are live or recorded, including public use of radios and television. Any playing of music for public reception needs a licence. This includes playing a radio or showing a TV programme as well as music transmitted over the internet. Currently (Summer 2009) the PRS is in discussion with public libraries about access to music, including that provided through the People's Network, as this may constitute broadcasting.

10.35 Mechanical Copyright Protection Society

The MCPS licenses the recording of music onto any medium and re-recording of music from abroad. Essentially, the MCPS licenses the making of a recording. The

PRS licenses the public performance of that music and PPL licenses the public use of the recording.

10.36 Phonographic Performance Ltd

PPL is a music industry collecting society representing over 2500 record companies, from the large multinationals to the small independents. It collects licence fees from broadcast and public performance users on behalf of the record companies. This licence fee revenue, after deduction of running costs, is then distributed to the record company members and to performers. Libraries and others should note that when a recording containing music is played in public, then royalties are due both to the PRS and to PPL, as one collects for the composers and musicians and the other for the recording company.

10.37 Motion Picture Licensing Corporation

The MPLC licenses the public performance of motion pictures. It represents over 80 producers and distributors and includes most major Hollywood studios as well as many independent ones. Any public performance requires a licence, including educational establishments when the material is not being used for instruction (see paragraphs 6.47–6.48). Note that nurseries and pre-school groups are not included in the definition of an educational establishment.

10.38 What about other licences?

There is an increasingly bewildering array of licences and permissions systems available. They include the JISC/PA guidelines and UK-wide HEFC licence; the NESLi2 (National E-Journals Initiative) and HERON (Higher Education on Demand). See Appendix 1 for contact details. Also, many individual publishers have their own tailor-made licences for different situations. It is impossible to do more than indicate that these exist and users should follow them up as necessary.

10.39 Other licences

There are various licences available from individual publishers who may license copying and reuse in both paper and electronic forms. Some are included in journal-pricing mechanisms which automatically give permission to make x number of copies, and almost all access to electronic publications is achieved with various and varying conditions attached which form a licence.

An increasing number of documents are now made available to the public via various collaborative online services such as Creative Commons, open access services and open archives.

10.40   **What is Creative Commons?**

Creative Commons is probably the best known alternative method of disseminating academic publications. Creative Commons licenses the copying, reuse, distribution, and in some cases, modification of the original owner's creative work without having to obtain permission every single time from the rights holder. Owners of the rights in documents made available through Creative Commons have to allow most of these uses, otherwise the objective of making documents more freely available is not achieved. Copyright owners tag their documents to show what uses are permitted, using a code system for ease of reference.

10.41   **So can material licensed under Creative Commons be used by anyone?**

Yes, and in any way indicated by the copyright owner.

10.42   **Are these the only ways documents can be used?**

Not necessarily. Contributors to Creative Commons can choose to be more generous and allow, for example, commercial use of their documents. There is even a code which allows the copyright owner to waive all rights so that the material can be used in any way at all.

10.43   **Is this legally binding or could a copyright owner complain about use of the material?**

The Creative Commons licence is considered binding as an agreement in English and Welsh law and as a contract in Scottish law. Provided you stick to the limits set by the copyright owner and observe any conditions, such as acknowledging the source, you are acting legally.

10.44   **What is open archives/access?**

Open access is a movement to make scholarly publications more readily available to the academic community. Various models exist. For example, an author may submit a paper for online publication and pay a fee for this. Access to the paper is then free for users, who do not need to subscribe to the conventional journal. Another model is that there is no fee but only those who contribute may gain access to the papers.

10.45 Does this mean that the papers can be freely copied and distributed?

No. Unless the copyright owner states to the contrary, the usual restrictions will apply.

These are just examples and others can be found and will emerge! However, the questions and answers given here are likely to be valid for any similar service.

Section 11
Computer programs, websites and the electronic world

11.1 What is the difference between electronic material and databases?

It is very important to distinguish between electronic material and databases. One is the format in which a work is stored or transmitted, the other is a form of a work itself. There are many works which are electronic but not databases and equally many databases that are not electronic! This chapter tries to deal with some of these questions but users of this book should realize that the situation is constantly changing and the subject matter, questions and answers are all moving targets. Because the term 'electronic materials' can cover works in electronic form, computer programs and databases these items will be dealt with separately in this chapter, under the usual headings, although they are all linked together in some respects.

11.2 Is copyright very different for electronic materials?

There are many copyright questions which arise in the electronic world to which the answers are exactly the same as in the more traditional, paper-based world. However, some issues are peculiar to electronic materials and some of the answers which are quite clear in the paper-based world are not so obvious when we deal with electronic materials. The introduction of specific legislation on databases makes many of the answers different if the work is considered a database.

Computer programs
11.3 Are computer programs a separate sort of work?

In some ways, but not in others. Although computer programs are classed as literary works, there are some special conditions which apply. They are literary works because the definition of a literary work is that it is 'written, spoken or sung and recorded in some notation or code'. Computer programs are a series of 0s and 1s, so this counts as a code which is recorded.

11.4   **What about computer programs which have been printed out?**

These are literary works. See Section 4.

11.5   **A lot of work goes into preparing the design of a computer program. Is that protected as well?**

It would in any case be considered as a literary work, but the law does specify this type of work as being protected.

11.6   **Who is the author of a computer program?**

The person who wrote the program.

11.7   **How long does copyright in a computer program last?**

The same as for a literary work (see Section 4).

11.8   **What rights does the copyright owner of a computer program have?**

Basically, the same as in a literary work (see Section 4).

11.9   **Are there any special rules?**

It is worth noting that translation of a computer program includes transferring it from one computer language to another. But see the following paragraph.

11.10   **Are computer programs subject to fair dealing?**

Yes, but just how this could work in practice is difficult to determine. One area where a sort of fair dealing exists is in allowing the translation of a lower-language program into a higher language. Strangely, the law excludes this activity under fair dealing but specifically allows it in another part of the legislation! This must be done by a lawful user of the program.

11.11   **What about making back-up copies?**

If a lawful user needs to make a back-up copy for lawful use of the program, then this is not an infringement of copyright. 'Lawful use' is not defined.

11.12   **Supposing a programmer wants to use the program to create a quite separate program? Can the program be decompiled for this purpose?**

Yes, provided that the necessary conditions are met. These are that the information obtained through decompiling the program is not used for any other purpose than creating an independent program which must not be similar to the one decompiled. In addition, the information must not be passed on to anyone unless they need to know for the purposes of creating the new program, nor must the information be readily available through any other source.

11.13 Sometimes contracts forbid some of the copying outlined in the previous paragraphs. Can anything be done?

Yes, the law specifically states that where a contract tries to prevent any of these actions, then that element of the contract is null and void.

Broadcasting

11.14 How does broadcasting apply to computer programs?

This is not really applicable to computer programs. Where a work is in electronic format the same rules apply as if it were in paper format.

Lending and rental

11.15 Can computer programs be lent or rented out?

They can be lent, other than by public libraries, but cannot be rented without the copyright owner's consent. See paragraphs 4.72–4.73.

Translation and adaptation

11.16 Is this right relevant to computer programs?

Yes. A specific clause in the law allows the translation of a lower-language program into a higher language.

Educational copying

11.17 Can computer programs be copied for educational purposes?

Only with the consent of the copyright owner directly or under licence. Some software is made available specifically for educational purposes and is free of copyright restrictions, provided that it is not exploited for commercial purposes. The exceptions for setting examination questions would seem to apply to computer programs as to other copyright works.

Library and archive copying

11.18   Can computer programs be copied by libraries and archives for their users?

No, unless it is possible to determine what is a reasonable proportion of a computer program, and it could then be copied for the reader as part of a non-periodical work (see paragraphs 4.182 and following and especially 4.204). In practice, the answer is simply 'no'.

11.19   What happens if the library has a computer program or other electronic material which becomes unusable for technical reasons? Can it be copied so that it can continue to be used?

Yes, provided that the conditions of purchase do not prohibit such copying and the original copy is not retained, otherwise it becomes an infringing copy.

Materials in electronic form

11.20   Are electronic materials defined in legal terms?

Yes. 'Electronic' means actuated by electric, magnetic, electromagnetic, electro-chemical or electromechanical energy, and 'in electronic form' means in a form usable only by electronic means.

11.21   So are electronic materials a separate group of protected works?

No. What is protected is the content of the electronic material and the electronic version of it. This is just like a paper copy, where the contents of a book are protected and the typography is protected separately.

11.22   But electronic materials always need some software to make them work. Is this part of the copyright in the work?

No. It is important to distinguish between the content of the work and the supporting computer systems. The latter will be copyright in their own right as computer software. It would be possible, for example, to have an electronic document which was out of copyright but software which was certainly still protected.

11.23   Are e-mails protected by copyright?

If the message meets the criteria for being eligible for copyright (original, fixed and from an appropriate country), then it is capable of being protected. Straightforward business messages merely confirming details of a contract or specification are probably not protected, as they are merely statements of fact, but messages which contain opinion or some form of original wording certainly are protected.

11.24 Can e-mails be sent on to other people?

Only if the person who sent it says so or it is generally understood to be the practice in the organization. While it is probably OK to send the message to someone else in the same organization to which it was sent, it certainly is not OK to send it to another outside organization or person.

Computer-generated works

11.25 Some works are generated automatically by computer, so who is the author of a computer-generated work?

The law says it is the person by whom the arrangements necessary for the creation of the work were undertaken.

11.26 Is it really possible for a work to be totally computer-generated?

This is open to debate. Although there are documents which can be generated automatically, somewhere along the line a human person set up the program to generate the work, or at least gave the computer some instructions on how this should subsequently be done.

11.27 How long does the copyright in a computer-generated work last?

The copyright in a computer-generated work expires 70 years from the end of the year in which the work was made. See 4.99 and following for the duration of copyright.

Authorship of electronic materials

11.28 Who is the author of an electronic work?

The author of the content of an electronic work will be decided in the same way as if that work were not electronic. In other words, if it is an electronic text, think of it as a book or periodical article, if it is a picture, consider whether it is a photograph or painting, and so on.

Moral rights

11.29   Do authors of electronic materials enjoy moral rights?

Yes, in exactly the same way as in other materials. But since it is unlikely that a book or film will be released only in electronic form the moral right to be named as the author in these two cases is equally unlikely to arise. However, the internet may be used to create artistic works where authors do have the right to have their name attached to a work when exhibited in public. Moral rights are very important in an electronic context. It is very easy to change content or authorship, or conceal the origin of a work in an electronic context and all of these are moral rights enjoyed by authors. Essentially, the same rules apply as for the paper world.

11.30   If the work is scanned or digitized who will be the author of the electronic version?

It is unlikely that the scanned or digitized version of a work will have an individual author. Unless one can specifically be identified, the electronic version will be considered anonymous and the rules for anonymous works will apply.

11.31   Does authorship really matter in electronic documents?

Yes, and it will become a vital issue. Researchers and users generally want to know who was responsible for a document, database or any other work, as this has a bearing on its importance and value. It also gives an idea of the point of view behind an author's work. It is also possible now to use technology to link authorship to payment. Anyway, those who write really do want the credit, even if there is no money involved.

Ownership

11.32   What are the rules for ownership of electronic works?

The rules for ownership of electronic works are the same as for materials in printed format.

11.33 **Do owners enjoy the same rights for electronic materials as they do for paper materials?**

Broadly, yes, but with some very important additions and one or two changes as outlined below.

11.34 **What about copying the work?**

This is an exclusive right of the owner.

11.35 **But surely every use of an electronic document involves copying? Does this mean that all such copying is an infringement?**

Fortunately not. The original 1988 Act gave the owner the exclusive right to control the making of transient or incidental copies even if these were essential to some legitimate use of the work. Thus, to call something up on a website would technically be an infringement as you cause the work to be copied to the Internet Service Provider (ISP) and then to your own hard disk. The legislation now prevents the copyright owner from enforcing copyright in such temporary copies provided that:

- they are a necessary part of the technical process to transfer the information
- the transfer is between third parties (i.e. website ISP end-user)
- the intended use is otherwise legal
- the temporary copy does not have any independent economic significance.

11.36 **What would constitute a copy with economic significance?**

The law does not say, but if you send someone a fax and the person receiving it prints it out immediately, then the intermediate digital copies are not significant. But if you stored the message so it could be retransmitted to lots of other people in your organization that would certainly have an independent economic significance.

11.37 **Who has the right to issue copies to the public?**

This is an exclusive right of the copyright owner and needs to be interpreted in the context of both online activity and physical carriers such as CD-ROMs or DVDs.

11.38 **Who has the right to perform, show or play the work?**

These rights are the same. Be aware that allowing something to be viewed by a number of people all at the same time is considered a performance by some copyright owners, and viewing by more than one person at a time is sometimes prohibited under some licences for electronic materials.

11.39   Who has the right to adapt or translate the work?

These rights are the same.

Lending and rental

11.40   Can electronic materials be rented?

Rental, as for all other copyright works, is an exclusive right of the copyright owner and this includes both works in electronic form and computer programs as such.

11.41   What about lending electronic materials?

From a legal point of view, both computer programs and works in electronic form can be lent. In practice, these products are usually sold with restrictions included in the contract so that they cannot be lent or used on premises other than those specified in the contract. If there is no specific contract, then it should be possible to lend, for example, a CD-ROM within the limits for lending specified in paragraphs 4.182 and following.

11.42   Supposing a library has a work in electronic form and another library wants to consult it. Can the second library be given access for a limited time?

Probably not. The contract giving access will define who can use a particular electronic work.

11.43   Is it meaningful to talk about lending in an electronic sense?

Yes, for two reasons. First, electronic materials may still be on physical carriers, such as disks, and these could be physically lent. Second, lending really consists of passing something to someone else so that the owner of it does not have use of it for a limited time while the other person does. This can now be achieved electronically by transmitting something to someone and (a) putting a 'block' on access to it while it is being used elsewhere and (b) constructing automatic erasing mechanisms so that the 'borrowing' library or person loses the work after the specified time. Watch out for developments in this area.

Publication right

11.44   Are electronic materials generally subject to publication right?

Theoretically, yes, but where do you find such materials out of copyright!?

Communication to the public

11.45   Is this right applicable to electronic materials?

This right was designed exclusively for electronic materials, so the answer is 'yes'! In a nutshell, it allows the copyright owner to control putting the work onto a website and thus plugs the hole in the law which excludes transmission of a website from the definition of a broadcast.

11.46   What is the actual definition of this right?

The definition of communication to the public right is:

- broadcasting the work
- making the work available by electronic transmission so that members of the public may access it from a place and at a time individually chosen by them.

Performance

11.47   Are the rights of performance relevant to electronic materials?

Yes, in two respects. First, the content of an electronic document may be multimedia in nature, with songs, speeches or dancing. These all have rights of performance in them. Second, performers now enjoy a separate right to prevent their performances being made available on the internet without their permission. This is called 'Making available right'.

11.48   What exactly is this right, then?

It is defined as: 'Right to prevent anyone making available to the public a recording of a performance by electronic transmission so that members of the public may access the recording from a place and at a time chosen by them.'

Duration

11.49 How long does copyright in an electronic work last?

So far as the content is concerned, the same rules apply as if the work were not electronic.

11.50 But if a new edition of a work causes a new term of copyright, what constitutes a new edition of an electronically stored work?

That is difficult to decide. Obviously if a whole new piece is added, then the work is a new edition, but if, as in the case of a database, material is added frequently and in small pieces, it is difficult to say whether every addition creates a new edition or whether a lot of new data has to be added before this can be claimed. A further problem is that no actual printed version will be made every time a change is made, so some editions may come and go and never be known about. Special rules apply to databases (see Section 9).

Fair dealing

11.51 Is there fair dealing in electronic works?

This is not an easy question to answer. Technically, there is fair dealing in the content of any electronic work where that content qualifies for fair dealing as a literary, dramatic, musical or artistic work. However, as electronic works can be accessed usually only by the use of passwords and a contract with the supplier, what can and cannot be done by a user is governed more by the terms of that contract and the issue of the password, than by copyright law as such. A further consideration is what is 'fair' in electronic terms. Fair dealing is not limited to copying, but this is the most usual form which it takes. But the idea of 'fair' (see paragraph 4.130 and following) may be difficult to justify in an electronic world when it is so easy to exactly reproduce a work, store and retransmit it and even change it. Whether fair dealing generally exists in an electronic world has never been tested. It should, but it may or may not, depending on the circumstances. The World Intellectual Property Organization (WIPO) – the body responsible for administering international copyright treaties – has supported the idea that fair dealing should exist in the electronic environment.

Educational use

11.52 Can electronic materials be used for educational purposes?

If they were acquired in electronic form, then only within the terms of any licence under which access to them has been negotiated. If no such licence exists, then the usual rules would apply (see paragraphs 4.164 and following). If they were originally in paper form and have been digitized, then they may be used in the same way as paper copies, provided the digitization was undertaken legally.

11.53 What about using electronic materials in VLEs or MLEs?

A group of students signing up for work done through a VLE environment should understand that any work they put up on the server can be used, modified or commented on by any other member of the VLE/MLE group. Retention of the work beyond the lifespan of the group would be an infringement. It would also be an infringement to put the work up on the internet or intranet site of the whole university/college, as this would be communicating the work to the public by electronic means.

11.54 What about putting theses or dissertations on the internet?

While this might be allowed for the text prepared by the student, the copyright in any copyright material included in the thesis as allowed for educational purposes (see paragraph 4.173) would be infringed and this should not be done except with the permission of the original copyright owner.

Other purposes

11.55 For what other purposes does fair dealing apply?

The law permits use of electronic materials for criticism or review and reporting current events in just the same way as other materials.

11.56 Are there any other limitations?

The rules for use of copyright materials for public administration and by visually impaired people are the same.

Protection mechanisms

11.57 **Some electronic documents can be accessed only by using a password or giving your credit card number. Is this legal?**

Yes, the law specifically protects the use of effective technological measures to protect electronic materials.

11.58 **What does 'effective technological measures' actually mean?**

If use of the work is controlled by the copyright owner through:

- an access control or protection process such as encryption, scrambling or other transformation of the work or
- a copy control mechanism which achieves the intended protection,

then the protection mechanism is considered an effective one.

11.59 **What difference does this make?**

A lot, because it is an offence (and this can be criminal) to circumvent such effective protection mechanisms, and the copyright owner has the same redress as if the copyright of the work itself were infringed.

11.60 **But this could stop someone from exercising the privileges they have under fair dealing or use by a VIP?**

Yes, this is true.

11.61 **What can be done in these circumstances?**

The law provides a very cumbersome and unsatisfactory remedy in these circumstances. In summary, this is what it says: If an effective technological measure prevents a user from benefiting from exceptions such as fair dealing, library privilege, needs as a VIP or educational copying, they shall make a complaint to the Secretary of State. The Secretary of State may give to the copyright owner or licensee such directions as seem fit to establish whether any voluntary measure of agreement already subsists enabling the complainant to benefit from the exceptions. This cumbersome procedure was under review as of Autumn 2009.

11.62 **Are there other protection mechanisms?**

Yes, the other mechanism is referred to as Electronic Rights Management System (ERMS).

11.63 What is an ERMS?

An ERMS is defined in law as 'any information provided by the copyright owner which identifies the work, the author or any other right holder, or information about the terms and conditions of use of the work, and any numbers or codes that represent such information'.

11.64 Is this data protected by law?

Yes, it is an offence to remove the data (which is usually encoded using metadata tags) or to transmit the document to a third party without the data.

Websites

11.65 Do websites present any particular problems?

Websites present all kinds of copyright problems. The paragraphs below give some indication of the problems libraries may face when considering using website technology to develop their services. You will need to consider who owns the website and whether the website constitutes a database as defined in law. Other issues include the status of a website (whether a broadcast or a cable programme service) and liability of website providers.

11.66 Is it an infringement to put works on the internet or world wide web?

Yes. This is infringing the right of communication of the work to the public by electronic means.

11.67 But supposing a document is put on the web but nobody ever downloads it. Is this still an infringement?

Yes, because the document has been made available to the public by electronic means. The fact that nobody accesses the work is another matter. It is an infringement of communication to the public right, even if this is done without charge, unless the person issuing the copies has the right to do so. The fact that nobody ever reads these copies is irrelevant!

11.68 Does the fact that it is so easy to build links to other websites pose any problems?

Possibly. It depends on whether you build your link to the homepage of the other website, build deep links (direct into the text of the other website), use framed links (which bring up a framed image which does not make clear whose property it actually is) or embed links (where an actual image from another website is embedded in your own to make the link direct). If you build a direct ('deep') link you should always give the user the option of finding the homepage as well.

11.69   Why go to so much trouble?

Because (a) the website owner may not wish his website to be associated with yours – you may be promoting views with which they strongly disagree; (b) you may bypass important information about ownership, conditions of use and even advertising, all of which the user would have found on the homepage; (c) if the user does not perceive that the information is owned by and made available through a different website provider from the one where the reader began the search, the reader may think the material is owned or supplied by the original website to which they logged on. This can cause the library to be accused of 'passing-off' – making services available which users think come from the library when, in fact, they belong to someone else.

11.70   Some websites have an icon to click for copyright information. Is this legal or necessary?

It is very necessary to ensure that users know exactly who owns what and what the user can do with material located. The icon prevents the user claiming ignorance of either ownership or conditions. Where websites start with a statement such as 'By clicking on this icon you agree that you have read the conditions of use and copyright statement', then the user is bound by those conditions and cannot plead ignorance.

11.71   Is all material on the web copyright?

Probably. To be safe, behave with material on the web as if it were in paper form. If you would not copy or distribute it in paper form, then do not do it in electronic form. That is, unless the owner specifically states that this can be done – which many website owners do.

11.72   What about older text, such as medieval manuscripts which have been put on the web by major libraries or archives?

The original text may be out of copyright but the electronic version will almost certainly attract its own copyright, as it will have been created as a result of extensive research, editing and correction. Electronic images are rarely in a sufficiently good state to be mounted without careful attention. This may mean that a new copyright work has been created (but see paragraph 2.3). In addition, most such websites probably qualify for protection as databases, as they should meet the definition of a database (see paragraph 9.1). They are pretty poor websites if they do not! So extraction and reuse of substantial parts of it would be excluded. However, if there is no copyright in the original material, then there is no infringement of the communication to the public right.

11.73 Do most copyright rules apply to websites or are there special issues to consider?

There are many copyright questions which arise in the electronic world to which the answers are exactly the same as in the more traditional, paper-based world. However, some issues are peculiar to electronic materials and some of the answers which are quite clear in the paper world are not so obvious when we deal with electronic materials. The legislation on databases makes many of the answers different if the work is considered a database.

Open Access

11.74 What is Open Access?

Open Access is defined by the Joint Information Systems Committee (JISC) of the universities as what 'occurs when full-text journal articles, plus other research information . . . are made freely available on-line'.

11.75 Does this mean that the material made available can be used in any way?

No. It simply means that access is free, but, unless otherwise stated, the material is protected just like any other copyright material and the usual rules apply.

Materials created by individuals on websites

11.76 There are lots of websites now where individuals can post their own writings, photos, videos or recordings of songs. Are these protected by copyright?

Yes. Anything that you create as an individual and put up on any of these sites, chatrooms or blogs is technically your property.

11.77 **Can I stop other people downloading and reusing it?**

By putting material onto these types of website you must be aware that other people will download this material and therefore it could be argued that you have given an implied licence for them to do this.

11.78 **Can they use my material to make their own postings or other works?**

No. That would be a clear infringement, especially if they actually published your photos, words or films.

11.79 **Supposing the video I post on one of these websites does contain copyright work from other people, such as songs, music playing in the background or even a photo of a painting?**

This is something you must try to avoid, because this infringes the copyright in the music, song or painting and also may infringe the performing rights of the musicians as well as the copyright in the recording. Similarly, any library or information service must be extremely careful if it downloads and circulates any material from these kinds of websites, as it may contain infringing material which could cause the service to be accused of illegally publishing the material and circulating it.

The following paragraphs list some of the more common websites (as at Summer 2009). Others are appearing all the time and it is important to check what each one says about copyright if you intend to make material available through it or use it as a source of information.

11.80 *MySpace*

MySpace, which is a social networking service, has a strict policy about the use of copyright material posted on its website. This states: 'The MySpace Services contain Content of Users and other MySpace licensors. Except as provided within this Agreement, you may not copy, modify, translate, publish, broadcast, transmit, distribute, perform, display, or sell any Content appearing on or through the MySpace Services.'

MySpace also prohibits the posting of any material that constitutes or promotes an illegal or unauthorized copy of another person's copyrighted work, such as providing pirated computer programs or links to them, providing information to circumvent manufacturer-installed copy-protect devices, or providing pirated music or links to pirated music files.

11.81   *YouTube*

YouTube is a video-sharing website where users can upload, view and share video clips. The website has copyright tips to help you avoid infringing. If material is found to be infringing, there is a proper procedure to notify YouTube that the material is infringing and should be taken down. Video clips are particularly vulnerable to including copyright material such as music and recordings, so take particular care when posting something and also when using anything you find on YouTube.

11.82   *Wikipedia*

Material on Wikipedia is protected by copyright but it is contributed under a licence which allows free use, provided that the subsequent use is also released for free. In other words, you cannot take substantial amounts of Wikipedia material and republish this commercially. Text in Wikipedia, excluding quotations, has been released under the GNU Free Documentation License (GFDL) (or is in the public domain), and can therefore be reused only if you release any derived work under the GFDL. This requires that, among other things, you attribute the authors and allow others to freely copy your work. If you want to reuse the material for commercial publication or put it on the internet with any form of protection mechanisms, then this material ceases to be licensed and becomes infringing. This is a summary, see the licence text for the exact details.

11.83   **Do Wikipedia authors have to sign up to these conditions?**

No, but by agreeing to contribute they give an implied licence to use their work under the GNU Free Documentation License. You cannot contribute to Wikipedia without agreeing to this.

11.84   *Flickr*

Flickr is a photo-sharing website which allows participants to share their photos with other members. Copyright remains with the photographer. If any participant considers that their work has been unfairly copied and reused or other intellectual property rights have been infringed, Flickr has an online complaint form through which action can be taken to have the member who has infringed barred or their material blocked.

11.85   *Facebook*

Facebook's mission is to give people the power to share and to make the world more open and connected, and to keep up with friends, upload an unlimited number of photos, share links and videos, and learn more about the people they meet. It is a requirement of membership of Facebook that, when you register, you guarantee not to infringe other people's copyright in the material you post or to use other people's copyright material in a way that would infringe their rights.

Section 12
Other matters

International treaties

12.1 **What importance does international copyright have?**

Technically there is no such thing as 'international copyright'. Each country has its own copyright laws, but most major countries belong to some or all of the three international conventions. Under these treaties and conventions each country protects the works produced in other countries as if they had been produced within its own borders, although usually works are not protected in a country for longer than they would be in the country of origin. So if a work is produced in a country where protection lasts for 50 years but is imported into a country where protection lasts for 70 years, then that work will still be protected for only 50 years in the country of importation.

12.2 **Which are these three major conventions?**

The Berne Copyright Convention, the Universal Copyright Convention and the Trade-Related Intellectual Property (TRIPS) element of the World Trade Agreement. A fourth, the WIPO Copyright Treaty, was agreed in 1996.

12.3 **Are there any countries which do not belong to any of these conventions?**

Yes, but the number is decreasing all the time. Those who have not signed one or more treaties cannot benefit from the liberalization of trade planned under the World Trade Agreement, so there is an incentive to reform or improve national copyright laws in most countries.

12.4 **If a country does not belong to one of these treaties does this mean that its publications can be copied?**

Perhaps. Although not all countries belong to one of the international treaties, one or two have signed bilateral agreements with the UK for mutual protection.

It is best to check the latest SI (see Section 1).

12.5 What is the importance of the copyright symbol?

The idea of the symbol is to indicate that the work is protected by copyright in the country of origin and has been registered for copyright protection. This is important under the Universal Copyright Convention, as publications without the symbol are not regarded as protected. As the USA has now joined the Berne Convention, under which no formality is required for registering a copyright document, the symbol is chiefly important on publications from those countries which belong to the UCC but not to Berne. It also protects publications in those same UCC countries, so it is important for publishers to include it on their works even if it is not required in the country of origin, as it should protect them when exported to UCC countries. Lack of the symbol has no significance in most countries.

Legal deposit

12.6 What is the connection between legal deposit and copyright law?

None, nor has there been for many years. Copyright deposit exists to enable the designated libraries to build up collections of the publicly available material produced in the UK. The law was radically revised in 2003, under the Legal Deposit Act 2003, which includes enabling legislation to protect and manage copyright for electronic materials deposited with the designated libraries.

12.7 Why do some people still call it 'copyright deposit'?

Because it used to be a prerequisite for being able to claim copyright. The law on legal deposit was enshrined in the Copyright Act of 1911, hence this misnomer has continued for many years. But international conventions do not require any formal deposit before claiming copyright. Copyright deposit should now really be called 'legal deposit'.

12.8 Is there a connection between PLR and copyright?

Yes. This was not true until the introduction of the lending/rental legislation, but PLR and copyright are now firmly linked. See paragraphs 4.72–73.

12.9   What is the connection between ISBNs, ISSNs and copyright?

Absolutely none. ISBNs, ISSNs and similar numbering systems are essentially tools of the bookselling and publishing industry which have been hijacked by librarians as useful systems for cataloguing, identifying and locating. Their presence or absence from a document has no bearing on its copyright status.

12.10   There has been a lot of talk about a right called 'droit de suite'. What is it?

Droit de suite is a right given to the creator of an original work of art (painting, sculpture, etc.) so that each time the work is sold the creator gets a percentage of the increased price, if there is one. This means that a painter who starts off as unknown and sells paintings for a few pounds can benefit from any subsequent fame achieved.

12.11   Does this have anything to do with libraries or archives?

Only if they have, or plan to acquire, collections of original works of art.

12.12   Has this right been introduced into the UK?

No, not yet. It was agreed by the European Parliament early in 1997 but it is still not effective in the UK.

Other legislation

12.13   Human rights laws in the UK guarantee individuals the right of free speech. They also protect family life and personal privacy. Can copyright be seen as infringing human rights?

No, because the assertion of the right of free speech cannot be used to take away private property from someone else. As copyright is a property law, this means you can express yourself in any legal way you wish, but not use someone else's property to do it. However, see paragraph 5.16 with important comments on photographs and privacy.

12.14   How does copyright interact with data protection?

Although most data covered by the Data Protection Act will be liable to database right, the rights conferred by the Data Protection Act do not change the rights of owners of database right at all.

12.15   What about freedom of information laws?

Again, rights of access to information do not change the rights of owners of the copyright in that information. Freedom does not mean it is delivered free of charge. See paragraphs 4.312–313 for more detailed information.

Appendix 1
List of useful addresses

Authors' Licensing and Collecting Society (ALCS)

The Writers' House
13 Haydon Street
London EC3N 1DB
For all general enquiries please contact:
Tel: 020 7264 5700
Fax: 020 7264 5755
E-mail: alcs@alcs.co.uk
Website: www.alcs.co.uk

British Copyright Council

29–33 Berners Street
London W1T 3AB
Tel: 01986 788 122
Fax: 01986 788 847
E-mail: secretary@britishcopyright.org
Website: www.britishcopyright.org

CILIP: the Chartered Institute of Library and Information Professionals

7 Ridgmount Street
London WC1E 7AE
Tel: 020 7255 0500
Fax : 020 7255 0501
E-mail: info@cilip.org.uk
Website: www.cilip.org.uk

Christian Copyright Licensing International

CCLI
Chantry House
22 Upperton Road
Eastbourne
East Sussex BN21 1BF
Tel: 01323 417711
Fax: 01323 436112
Website: www.ccli.co.uk

The Copyright Licensing Agency Ltd

Saffron House
6–10 Kirby Street
London EC1N 8TS
Tel: 020 7400 3100
Fax: 020 7400 3101
E-mail: cla@cla.co.uk
Website: www.cla.co.uk

Design and Artists Copyright Society

33 Great Sutton Street
London EC1V 0DX
Tel: 020 7336 8811
Fax: 020 7336 8822
E-mail: info@dacs.org.uk
Website: www.dacs.co.uk

Educational Recording Agency

New Premier House
150 Southampton Row
London WC1B 5AL
Tel: 020 7837 6222
Fax: 020 7837 3750
E-mail: era@era.org.uk
Website: www.era.org.uk

HERON

Website: www.heron.ingenta.com/

HMSO Copyright Section

St Clements
Colegate
Norwich NR3 1BQ
Tel: 01603 521000
Fax: 01603 723000
Website: (general) www.hmso.gov.uk

Ministry of Defence

Hydrographic Department
Finance Section
Ministry of Defence
Taunton
Somerset TA1 2DN
Tel: 01823 337900

Motion Picture Licensing Corporation

MPLC House
4 Saffrons Road
Eastbourne
East Sussex BN21 1DQ
Tel: 01323 649 647
Fax: 01323 439 354

Music Publishers' Association

6th Floor, British Music House
26 Berners Street
London W1T 3LR
Tel: 020 7580 0126
Fax: 020 7637 3929
E-mail: info@mpaonline.org.uk
Website: www.mpaonline.org.uk

National e-Journals Initiative (NESLi2)
Website: www.nesli2.ac.uk/

Newspaper Licensing Agency
Wellington Gate
Church Road
Tunbridge Wells TN1 1NL
Tel: 01892 525 273
Fax: 01892 525 275
E-mail: copy@nla.co.uk
Website: www.nla.co.uk

Ordnance Survey
Copyright Branch
Romsey Road
Maybush
Southampton SO9 4DH
Tel: 08456 05 05 05
Fax: 023 8079 2615
Website: www.ordsvy.gov.uk

Ordnance Survey Northern Ireland (OSNI)
[now part of Land & Property Services of Northern Ireland]
1st Floor, Lincoln Building
27–45 Great Victoria Street
Malone Lower
Belfast BT2 7SL
Website: www.lpsni.gov.uk

Performing Right Society
29–33 Berners Street
London W1T 3AB
Tel: 020 7580 5544
Fax: 020 7306 4455
Website: www.prs.co.uk

Phonographic Performance Ltd
> 1 Upper James Street
> London W1F 9DE
> Tel: 020 7534 1000
> Fax: 020 7534 1111
> E-mail: info@ppluk.com
> Website: www.ppluk.com

Public Lending Right Office
> Richard House
> Sorbonne Close
> Stockton-on-Tees TS17 6DA
> Tel: 01642 604699
> Fax: 01642 615641
> Website: www.plr.uk.com

Appendix 2
Selected sources of further information

Some useful books, journals and websites are listed below. An unofficial consolidated version of the CDPA can be found at www.ipo.gov.uk/cdpact1988.pdf. Several legal publishers also produce consolidated Acts, e.g. Sweet & Maxwell, Butterworths, Blackwells. When looking for books on copyright, note the publication date of the latest edition, as this will reflect how up-to-date the information actually is.

Books

Armstrong, C. J. and Bebbington, Lawrence W. (eds) (2004) *Staying Legal: a guide to issues and practice affecting the library, information and publishing sectors*, 2nd edn, London, Facet Publishing. ISBN 978-1-85604-438-7.

Burrell, R. and Coleman, A. (2005) *Copyright Exceptions: the digital impact*, Cambridge University Press, ISBN 978-0-52184-726-1.

Cornish, Graham P. (2003) *Keep it Legal: copyright guidance for school library staff*, Swindon, School Library Association. ISBN 1-903-44621-X.

Flint, Michael F. (2006) *A User's Guide to Copyright*, 6th edn, Tottel Publishing. ISBN 1-845-92068-6.

Garnett, Kevin et al. (2009) *Copinger and Skone-James on Copyright*, 15th edn (2 vols), London, Sweet & Maxwell. ISBN 978-1-84703-128-0. The copyright bible.

Laddie, Hugh et al. (2000) *The Modern Law of Copyright and Designs*, 3rd edn (3 vols), London, Butterworths. ISBN 0-406-90383-2. Although this appears rather dated it is invaluable for interpreting case law.

Padfield, Tim (2007) *Copyright for Archivists and Records Managers*, 3rd edn, London, Facet Publishing. ISBN 978-1-85604-604-6.

Pedley, Paul (2008) *Copyright Compliance*, London, Facet Publishing. ISBN 978-1-85604-640-4.

Pedley, Paul (2006) *Essential Law for Information Professionals*, 2nd edn, London,

Facet Publishing. ISBN 978-1-85604-552-0. Covers a wide range of legal issues, of which copyright is just one.

Pedley, Paul (2007) *Digital Copyright*, 2nd edn, London, Facet Publishing. ISBN 978-1-8560-608-4.

Pedley, Paul (ed.) (2005) *Managing Digital Rights: a practitioner's guide*, London, Facet Publishing. ISBN 978-1-85604-544-5.

Phillips, Jeremy (2005) *Butterworths Intellectual Property Law Handbook*, 5th edn, London, Butterworths. ISBN 1-405-70898-0.

Secker, Jane (2010) *Copyright and E-learning*, London, Facet Publishing. ISBN 978-1-85604-665-7.

Stokes, Simon (2003) *Art and Copyright*, Oxford, Hart Publishing. ISBN 978-1-84113-385-0.

Wienand, Peter, Booy, Anna and Fry, Robin (2000) *A Guide to Copyright for Museums and Galleries*, London, Routledge. ISBN 978-0-415-21721-7.

Periodicals

Copyright Bulletin. Published quarterly by Unesco, Paris. Archival issues accessible free online.

Copyright World. Published six times a year by Intellectual Property Publishing, London. Archival issues accessible free online.

European Intellectual Property Review. Published monthly by Sweet & Maxwell.

Managing Information. Published by Aslib, London. Has useful news and newsletter sections. Available online to subscribers.

Websites

www.copyrightcircle.co.uk
Contact for advice and training on copyright.

www.cilip.org.uk/policyadvocacy/copyright/advice/default.htm
The website for the Library and Archive Copyright Alliance, which brings together most of the major players in the information provision industry to discuss copyright.

www.ipo.gov.uk
A website maintained by the Patent Office to give information on a wide range of intellectual property issues. Copyright is well covered and there is a Frequently Asked Questions page.

www.wipo.int

To keep up with international developments in the World Intellectual Property Organization.

www.eblida.org

Useful for European developments, especially relating to libraries.

www.courtservice.gov.uk

Gives official transcripts of major cases. Searchable by subject.

www.bbc.co.uk/news

Surprisingly useful for latest news on copyright, especially in the media.

www.opsi.gov.uk/advice/crown-copyright/index.htm

Latest information on use of Crown copyright material.

www.cla.co.uk

The website for the Copyright Licensing Agency.

www.nla.co.uk

The website for the Newspaper Licensing Agency.

www.alcs.co.uk

The Authors' Licensing and Collecting Society website has links to all other licensing agencies in the UK.

Appendix 3
Statutory declaration forms

FORM A

DECLARATION: COPY OF ARTICLE OR PART OF PUBLISHED WORK

To:

The Librarian of .... Library

[Address of Library]

Please supply me with a copy of:

       *the article in the periodical, the particulars of which are [   ]

       *the part of the published work, the particulars of which are [   ]

required by me for the purposes of research or private study.

2.   I declare that:

    (a)   I have not previously been supplied with a copy of the same material by you or any other librarian;

    (b)   I will not use the copy except for research for a non-commercial purpose or private study and will not supply a copy of it to any other person; and

    (c)   to the best of my knowledge no other person with whom I work or study has made or intends to make, at or about the same time as this request, a request for substantially the same material for substantially the same purpose.

3.   I understand that if the declaration is false in a material particular the copy supplied to me by you will be an infringing copy and that I shall be liable for infringement of copyright as if I had made the copy myself.

†Signature ....

Date ....

Name   ....

Address   ....

              ....

              ....

*Delete whichever is inappropriate.

†This must be the personal signature of the person making the request. A stamped or typewritten signature, or the signature of an agent, is NOT acceptable.

FORM B

DECLARATION: COPY OF WHOLE OR PART OF UNPUBLISHED WORK

To:

The *Librarian/Archivist of .... *Library/Archive

[Address of Library/Archive]

Please supply me with a copy of:

the *whole/following part [particulars of part] of the [particulars of the unpublished work] required by me for the purposes of research or private study.

2. I declare that:

(a) I have not previously been supplied with a copy of the same material by you or any other librarian or archivist;

(b) I will not use the copy except for research for a non-commercial purpose or private study and will not supply a copy of it to any other person; and

(c) to the best of my knowledge the work had not been published before the document was deposited in your *library/ archive and the copyright owner has not prohibited copying of the work.

3. I understand that if the declaration is false in a material particular the copy supplied to me by you will be an infringing copy and that I shall be liable for infringement of copyright as if I had made the copy myself.

†Signature ....

Date ....

Name   ....

Address   ....

              ....

              ....

*Delete whichever is inappropriate.

†This must be the personal signature of the person making the request. A stamped or typewritten signature, or the signature of an agent, is NOT acceptable.

Index